CW00449355

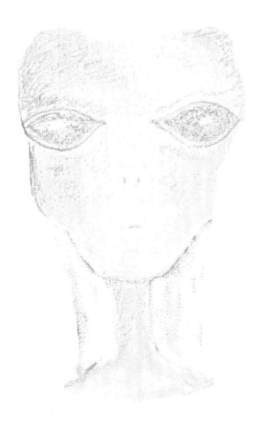

Dogged Days

The strange life and times of a child from eternity
Paranormal experiences with
Extraterrestrials, Humans,
& Beings from other dimensions

Ellis Taylor

BiggyBoo Books
Tis the buzz word in books

Black & White edition
ISBN: 978-0-9556861-2-2

Second edition: January 2009

First edition: December 2008

Colour edition
ISBN: 978-0-9550417-2-3

Published by
BiggyBoo Books
PO Box 23
Wheatley
OXFORD
OX33 1FL

www.biggyboo.com

The information in this book contains material of a general nature that is intended to complement, not replace, personal advice from your own physician. The author cannot accept responsibility for any difficulties arising from your failure to seek appropriate advice from your medical practitioner.

for
my children
&
my grandchildren

Foreword

There are few writers, particularly in the realm of the paranormal, where you feel that you are a part of their journey, as though you are inside their head as they write down the words you are reading. Ellis C Taylor is one of those people. He writes from the heart and that shows on every page of every book he has written. He calls a spade a spade and leaves the reader to decide whether or not to believe him.

Having spent a lifetime dealing with bizarre circumstance, Ellis is supremely qualified to write about the subject. In Dogged Days, he does just that, taking us on a personal voyage from childhood to the present, cataloguing events that range from witnessing UFOs to ghostly manifestations to coming face-to-face with a gnome – yes, a gnome! – and coming to terms with alien abduction. Some of the things of which he writes appear fantastical, but his sincerity shines through and you find yourself saying, "Wow!" as his story unfolds.

Armed with photographs, diary entries and accounts from friends and family, Dogged Days is a fabulous book, written in Ellis' usual, witty, self-deprecating style and should take pride of place on anybody's bookshelf.

Steve Johnson
UFO Data Magazine
6th November 2008

Other books by Ellis C. Taylor:

Living in the Matrix
In These Signs Conquer
The Esoteric Alphabet

About the Author

Ellis Taylor is a 7th son of Australia who was born on a 777 date on the western slope of a hill in *Bridget* country, next to the Blackwood River in south-west Australia. He is a great, great, grandson of the two eldest of the 9 sons of William and Margaret Forrest who landed in Western Australia from Scotland in 1842. The fourth and seventh child of each married in 1908. The numbers 4, 7 and their sum, 11 and factors are integral frequency patterns in his life. Ellis' great, great, great uncle John (later Lord Forrest) was a famous explorer, who became premier of Western Australia and acting Prime Minister of Australia another uncle was also a noted explorer and a mayor of Perth. Both are commemorated in the city landscape of Perth and several other places around Western Australia.

At two-years-old his family transferred to Oxford in England where his father was brought up. At first he stayed with his father's parents close to the Radcliffe Observatory, an edifice that is reputed to be an entrance to the Underworld with its main entrance oriented south and governed by Cancer. Ellis was christened at the nearby St. Giles Church and attended St. Barnabas nursery school in Jericho. Several key places in Ellis' life are situated on a straight alignment that includes the Radcliffe Observatory, St. Giles church and Wadham College chapel as well as a number of other personally significant sites mentioned in his books.

His family were one of the first to move on to what became the then largest council housing estate in England, Blackbird Leys and he attended primary school there. The house where Ellis lived was right on the edge of the estate and only a matter of yards to fields, streams and ancient hedges - a long sacred landscape destined to be the set for numerous adventures, both earthly and *supernatural*. He remembers his childhood vividly; and with great affection and gratitude.

From the energetic, inspiring Blackbird Leys Primary School Ellis went to grammar school. At Southfield Grammar, Ellis excelled at cross-country running and bunking off; he enjoyed English, history, geography, sport, art and woodwork but his real forte there was daydreaming.

Burdened with 5 'O' levels and a bruised imagination he sleepwalked into a totally unsuitable apprenticeship as a buyer by way of an IQ exam that he trance sat and creamed. While still an apprentice he was the youngest assistant buyer in the giant British Leyland Corporation. One day he woke up and couldn't stand it anymore. They awarded him his apprenticeship anyway.

For several years Ellis was a part-time male model and eventually settled into running his own interior specialist decorating business. He also lectured in painting and decorating and decorative painting techniques at the Oxford College of Further Education.

Ellis went to live in Australia in 1991 but returned to the Isles regularly for 3 month periods almost every year. He still spends his time between both countries.

Ellis is self-taught through self-experience and as well has studied Tarot, numerology, hypnotism and alternative healing. He is an acknowledged psychic, a writer, a numerologist, and an unorthodox explorer into the mysteries of life.

www.biggyboo.com
www.ellisctaylor.com
www.oxfordtalks.com/ellistaylor.html

Front cover illustration
By Neil Hague

"It was as dark as hell. . .A large black dog, with eyes that looked back to before the dawn of everywhere, rose up and began to chew on my fingers"

www.neilhague.com

Testimonials

Before publishing this book proper I produced a limited edition pre-publication and asked several fellow *otherworld* travellers, researchers and writers to comment upon it. This initial draft book did not have as many accounts and photographs as this one does and it also had a plain black cover. Their comments which I have reproduced below are based on this version. My thanks go to each and every one of them.

'Paranormal events rarely touch many people's lives, but in others they seem to be commonplace - so I am pleased that Ellis Taylor has made his combined blogs over the past twelve years, as well as several other incidents, into a single narrative. I have discussed with him and attempted to analyse what has happened during an "abduction" or "missing time" experience, which Ellis has experienced fairly frequently. What's behind it all remains an enduring mystery. Many take the view that "aliens" are responsible - that is if you are a devotee of Ufology and attend the occasional conference. No doubt the religious would think this is the work of the Devil, demons or even God! Hard line materialists would suggest the victim is fantasy prone and converts mundane events into covert agendas purely for self-aggrandisement.

My own work involving fine dowsing techniques suggests that certain vulnerable people are susceptible to attack from various energy forms that exist all around us. Many of these are created as a bi-product of modern technology and "mental detritus" from human minds. No doubt Wilhelm Reich's discovery of "orgone" energy over 50 years ago is highly relevant. My indications are that the vulnerable subjects have fine openings or portals in their skulls which allow some of their personal energy or "spirit" to be exposed to the outside of their bodies. This leakage is then readily linked up with invasive energies which are drifting around in the atmosphere. The combined result is that the victim experiences feeling of horror, hallucinates or even goes through an "abduction" process.

Ellis Taylor has reported some of his most harrowing experiences after attending UFO conferences. Of course kindred spirits who have experienced something similar to Ellis tend to congregate at these shows. As well as swapping stories - they swap energies! If half-a-dozen *vulnerables* or more are in the same audience then they may take home more than they arrived with! Dowsing around Ellis when he reports bad vibes often reveals plumes of energy snaking round his head. I endeavour to remove these where possible. Often I have found pockets of energy in his car which might explain some of the missing time experiences he has recorded in this book while driving.

Much of this is pure guesswork - what happens when an invasive energy combines with the victim's own energies is impossible to resolve except for the anecdotal evidence produced by the person involved. Ellis has endeavoured to write down his experiences just as they happened here which goes a long way to explaining things and helping others. For my part I would like to establish how many people fall into the "vulnerable" category and offer protection if possible. It cannot be too jolly living with these "demons" or whatever you wish to name it. Read the text and should you be troubled or had similar experiences to those described - get in touch.

Geoff Ambler,
Vice-President, Contact International UFO Research
http://contactinternationalufo.homestead.com

Ellis has a wonderful way of writing; he makes things simple; easy to understand; but most of all he speaks (and writes) straight from the heart.

Some of the subjects he tackles aren't that easy to write about, but he's very uncomplicated and professional in the way he does write about them. There's no confusion; no waffling; he gets straight to the point and tells it as it is and I for one find that refreshing.

Most of all, he portrays the truth as he knows it to be and that is quite something in these troubled times.

An accomplished author, his works are a proverbial breath of fresh air guaranteed to dispel any cobwebs lodging in your mind!

Ann Andrews
Author of 'Walking Between Two Worlds, Belonging to None' and
Co-Author of 'Abducted, the True Story of Alien Abduction in Rural England'
www.walkingbetweenworlds.co.uk

Dogged Days is a book written on a human level in a simple style. It tells the story of a man like any other, someone you can identify with and sympathize with, but one who walks a tightrope suspended between this universe and others unseen that burst our lives out of the illusion that we've been told is the One Sole Reality. What he has experienced is real. Other people around him have witnessed some of the strangeness that he is involved in, including myself. His experiences made me laugh, they made me cry, and above all they made me *wonder*! Hopefully they will make you wonder too.

Ben Emlyn-Jones,
Author of the blogs, HPANWO and HPANWO Voice

Dogged Days testifies not only to one person's extraordinary experiences, but also to the reality of the hidden realms from which those experiences derive. Ellis is a committed researcher, and peerless guide to the weird; and this book is an authentic glimpse into his magical world.

Ben Fairhall
Researcher and Author of the website: 'Battling the Behemoth'
http://ben-fairhall.blogspot.com

Having known Ellis for a number of years and having shared various orb-hunting excursions, dowsing at sacred sites and been present with him, both here and in the USA, to experience first-hand some of the events he describes in his book, I have no hesitation in recommending this as an essential read for those who seek to understand a bit more about the true nature of reality. Ellis proved to me on several occasions that he can not only photograph orbs but can also see them. I consider him a dear and long-standing friend; a fellow traveller on a journey into the unknown.

Mike Oram
Creator of the cartoon strip 'Ben's World'
Author of 'Does It Rain In Other Dimensions?'
www.inotherdimensions.com

Like many thousands of people on this planet, Ellis Taylor lives in the tension betwixt and between two realities. There is the 'normal', everyday world where a living must be earned, the mundane minutiae of life attended to and where the 'supernatural' is a generally avoided topic and then there is the reality where other dimensions, off-world visitors, government black ops, frequency fluxes and energy portals are all too real and intrusive. Functioning in the former while experiencing the latter requires mental and emotional equilibrium, nerves of steel, an open mind, discernment and wisdom and a brave heart. Ellis has all of these and more. Especially he has the courage to tell his story and thereby add more pieces to the jigsaw of the true nature of reality. Apart from all that, he is a really nice person and his book is interesting!

Fran Pickering
Author of 'The Encyclopaedia of Animals in Nature, Myth and Spirit'
'The Pocket Pals' series
'The Super Secret Code Book'
and many other books for children.
www.inotherdimensions.com

From the moment we met Ellis we recognised him as a kindred spirit - and his new book, 'Dogged Days', is very much a book of the time.

It reflects issues and questions which will be familiar to many people, who have encountered the extraordinary. All such encounters cause us to re-evaluate our life and purpose here - and yet it is not so much what happens to us that is important but how we respond to those events, as confusing as they may sometimes be. Many people may claim to know all the Answers - but invariably those who do, usually haven't understood the questions in the first place.

In Dogged Days, Ellis candidly relates his own unusual experiences and in doing so draws alongside all who are less interested in popular answers and more concerned with asking the right questions about the nature of Reality.

John Pickering
Writer/Author of: 'One For The Road', 'Luminescence' and 'Beyond Photography'
www.lights2beyond.com

I have known Ellis for over 11 years and he has become a wonderful friend and a fellow researcher for whom I have deep respect. I met Ellis when he and his family were experiencing anomalous phenomena, i.e. contact with non-human intelligences. He had been led to my door by a joint friend, and said to me that there was no support group for this experience, and that *people just thought you were a 'loony'*. Although at that time I had not supported anyone with such experiences, I was aware of the phenomenon. On meeting Ellis I was in no doubts that this profound experience was impacting quite tangibly on both him and his family.

In fact I can honestly say that Ellis and his story provided a new direction and the catalyst for the creation of ACERN to support those with contact.

But even more importantly Ellis has shown tremendous courage in uncovering the hidden and 'darker side on this planet; a challenging task that would cast fear into most hearts. But I once asked Ellis if he would ever stop doing this given the forces he challenges?

His answer was no, they have killed me before for doing this but it is fundamental to my purpose and if they did do it again then I would just keep coming back and doing it again until I succeed! "

That is a man who has the honesty and integrity to do what he believes, and to speak his truth. I am honoured to be his friend.

Mary Rodwell
ACERN - The Australian Close Encounters Resource Network
Author of 'Awakening, How ET Contact can change your life'.
www.acern.com.au

Prepare to be taken on an enchanting journey of mystery and multi-dimensional exploration! To read Dogged Days is akin to being granted a private audience with a bard of ancient Albion, as Ellis Taylor engagingly weaves his-story with natural skill and charm. If ever there was a book to be read next to a roaring fire by candlelight, this is it...

Karen Sawyer
Author of Soul Companions and The Dangerous Man
www.soulcompanions.org

Author's Note

I have written this book to attest and to demonstrate that interactions with other *worlds* and *unseen* realities, and of course their inhabitants, are a natural human experience; more than that they participate, as we do, in providing vital faculties for unending expression through the infinite scope and limited facets of Creation's ambitions.

I want people who have remarkable experiences that convention denies and the orthodox scorn to know that in the great cast of Creation they are not the strange or gullible ones; that they are not alone and that what they have experienced is crucial.

I want people to believe in themselves, and the power of their own experiences. I want people to remember who they are, what they are, where they have come from and where they have been. I want them to appreciate the mysterious personal synchronicities and connections that ripple quietly, and loudly sometimes, many times every day. In every way I want them to notice their life.

To assist those who research these matters I have attempted to be as forthright as possible and to give as many personal details as I can, because it may be that such information collated from 'experiencers' offers them significant clues to why some of us have these so called extraordinary experiences and some do not.

Whatever your reasons are for reading this book I hope you find it informative, entertaining and inspiring. Thank you so much for being here, and for being interested.

Ellis Taylor 24th January 2009
SYDNEY

CONTENTS

A missing two hours
On the road again
Arrival
A most terrible night
Healing
Shadow walking
A green hill far away
Rumble in the jungle
Ghost dogs
Craik's in time
SkyBow
The Kirkstone Pass Inn
Past lives
Underworld entrance
Goodwill hunting?

PROBE International
Death lie silence
David Kelly
Blue light
Cornwall UFO Group Conference
International UFO Congress, Laughlin, Nevada
Report from Saturn's Underpants
Sages of Aquarius
Bulletins
I've got one!
A thousand small wings beating
Marks of my ancestors
Sidh-n-ey perhaps?
Reptilians
Probe conference October 2008
An Angel in our midst
Visions
Claremont
A day and a half
Sarah Payne
Remote control

INTRODUCTION

This book deals mainly with my own personal experiences of communions and contacts with beings that usually reside in alternative realities to the ones that our 5 physical senses can perceive.

Such interactions with *otherworlds* have been going on since the dawn of the human being and though the names we have for the visitors and the visited may be many and varied the essential aspects of the experiences are too alike to dismiss with airy certainty and textbook infallibility. It is very difficult to write effectively about one's knowledge and research into this subject without upsetting apple carts so I just write it down knowing that it is too important not to.

Some people attract attention from *otherworlds* while there are others that never will. Embedded in the DNA of some of us is a weaving sequence of 'code' that under the right circumstances triggers an ability to traverse dimensions. It isn't always awakened and many go through their whole lives unaware of this latent sequence - some of them ardent sceptics of anything *paranormal*.

It isn't a secret to our leading authorities though and it hasn't been for thousands of years. Several times, throughout history and up till the present day, the *Darkness Invisible* (the *Darkness*) - the little perceived evil force intent on the total destruction of this world and all of its inhabitants - has ordered the destruction of huge numbers of people sometimes just to prevent the birth of one child or to curtail the life of one that escaped the prevailing net; for, it is known that a time has to come when *the Wheel of Destiny* will turn and at that moment then will come 'the one'. 'The one' will succeed and it is to forestalling this that the *Darkness* devotes its accursed eye. We can count missing, abused and murdered children, so-called *serial-killer* cases, the *Dark* atrocities against native peoples, races and religions using all manner of excuses and of course the biblical destructions.

I haven't been told how this all began, or I can't remember, but I do know that these dragon lines (lights) in the blood are carried in particular families but that not every member of that family can be attuned to the same degree. At the most it will be only one child in a generation, sometimes out of several generations, who is capable of the inexorably exacting standards required by our champions, our guardians, those who are charged by Creation with the responsibility of ensuring that human beings on Earth are given every opportunity to survive and flourish. A deep understanding of this within humanity, mis-shaped by prevailing influences, has evoked the eldest male child preferential heir system adopted especially among the so-called elite classes; but, these bloodlines exist in every race and level of society, and 'the one' may be male or female. In my culture they are known as 'the Albi-gens' - pronounced (without coincidence) similarly to Albion - 'Albi-on'.

Many writers have got very close to this in recent years especially, for instance, Laurence Gardner in 'Bloodline of the Holy Grail' and 'Realm of the Ring Lords' where he names several dragon-light carriers. He is right, up to a point, but, and I strongly suspect that he knows this; the most potent carriers have traversed the ages, many lifetimes necessarily unacknowledged, kept safe, strengthening the ring current, hidden deep in the forest - or 'the Forrests', in my case, I have been told. It is relevant here to mention something I go into in my book, IN THESE SIGNS CONQUER, that is, that 'trees' are ancient metaphors for 'stars'; woods and forests for constellations and galaxies.[1]

There are extraordinary numbers of energetically-enhanced humans - Albi-gens and their counterparts - who have purposely incarnated for this run up to the energetic changes that accompany the Precession of the (Astrologically-marked) Ages - all of them observed (and occasionally retuned) by *otherworld beings* charged with this mission - as well as, of course, those who wish to disrupt it, either because they don't understand or that they understand very well and are threatened by it.

And that's as far as I'm going with this in this book because first I want to demonstrate, using my own experiences, that we really are NOT ALONE.

---

[1] 'Dragon -light' refers to fire in the flow, the genetic stream.

Forrest Family Coat-of-Arms showing the 7 oak trees upon the Fairy Hill portal.
Motto: '*While they are green they flourish*'
In These Signs Conquer: www.biggyboo.com/signs.html

One
DRAGONS ORBS & SHADOWS

I was driving towards Long Sutton in Lincolnshire en route to stay with my friends Paul and Ann Andrews.

Even for a seasoned *otherworld* traveller like me the months prior to this journey had been unusual. Orbs and coloured lights increasingly flashed around my country cottage, middle-of-the-night telephone calls on landline and mobile that when

Paul and Ann Andrews

answered only gave out peculiar sounds, or sometimes nothing at all. Concluding one international conversation with a friend in Australia an American voice sinisterly cut in with his own: 'Bye now!' [2]

Emails, scores of them, failed to arrive. Someone had been in my home; I noticed things missing, significant things mostly. My mobile phone *went walkabout* for nearly 3 months (and then turned up in a place that I regularly searched through – the door pocket of my car), a

strikingly aromatic piece of palisander wood that Peruvian shaman, Inti Caesar had given to me and safely stored documents also vanished. Then there were the *shadow people*, who sometimes walked past my windows, and inside my home, in daylight and at night time - and it wasn't just me who saw them either. I would regularly hear knocking on my windows at night but there was never anybody there. Sometimes flashlights would shine through the back windows. I frequently heard garbled voices inside my home; two mystified visitors heard them as well.

My neighbours told me that they heard unusual sounds coming from my house when I was away and joked that there must be a noisy ghost. I

---

[2] A month or so later I was speaking on the phone again with this friend. I mentioned what had been said at the end of our previous phone call (they hadn't heard it). At the end of the call another intrusive voice - this time in a rather posh English accent - cut in with: 'Cheerio!' I waited for them to add *'old bean'* but he didn't say it. Perhaps he will next time.

began to arrange things inside when I left so that I would be able to tell if there had been any intruders – and these confirmed there had been at first. Later these devices remained undisturbed but my neighbours continued to hear things being moved around and no one saw anyone entering or leaving my house. My home was very secure and the only entry point without making one hell of a noise is through the front door, which is open to view and easy to see from other properties.

Vehicles would pull up outside my cottage at all sorts of hours and stay there for a while. Now and again there would be a car sitting outside, with either one or sometimes two occupants, when I left for work. A couple of times a stranger, an old man, would be sitting on the park bench across the green and watch me intently as I drove away early in the morning. One night I arrived home just after  midnight and saw the silhouette of what looked like a shaven-headed man walk past my front window, but within the house. When I got inside nobody was there.

The ancient cottage, built before Columbus set eyes on *the New World*, straddles a weaving *Dragon Line* that links with the famous 'St. Michael'  Ley Line. Orbs regularly appeared in photos taken both inside and outside the house; many, many of them contained scenes and faces. One particular spot is really potent (see page 28) and it regularly affected unsuspecting visitors when I lived there. One morning I noticed dark finger marks above the doorway in this spot (left).

I traced the energy stream through the front garden - it had swept across the former site of an ancient pond, weaved sharply and struck straight through the front door to 'the spot'.

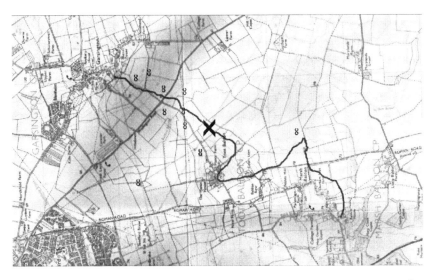

The St. Michael Line between Marsh Baldon and Garsington in Oxfordshire. [3]

[3] The 'St. Michael Line' is one of two intertwining energy lines (the other is The 'St. Mary Line') that weave across the widest part of Britain and marry precisely with the rising sun of Beltane (c. 5th May) and Lugnasadh (c. 5th August) - Celtic names for rites as old as humankind calculated by the position of the sun (15° Taurus and 15° Leo respectively).

I have tracked the *St. Michael Line* from the village church of 'St. Peter' in the Oxfordshire village of Marsh Baldon to the church of 'St. Mary' in Garsington village. Crop Circles gravitate on and around it most years. www.ellisctaylor.com/marshbaldontogarsington.html

For pioneering work regarding faces and scenes in orbs please visit Jane McCarthy's website: www.psychicinvestigators.net and John Pickering and Katie Hall's www.lights2beyond.com

Top: The vortex in my home outlined in orbs.
Below: Before and after - or rather after and *before* in this case: In December 2007 I
visited Rochester Cathedral and snapped this rather haunting portal in action at the
North Quire Transept and Pilgrim Steps
www.ellisctaylor.com/pokinroundrochester.html

Two
Out of Time & Place

I t was late September, and getting on for 2 o'clock in the afternoon, and I was driving on the A43 road near Silverstone when suddenly the thought came into my head that I ought to stop at a service station to visit the loo - just in case I encountered traffic hold-ups . . . Everything is now a blur before and after what happened next.

As I drove up the slope into the service station it struck me how it was unusually empty for such a busy time on a main road. Way up the far end of the parking area, near the motel, was a couple of cars but there were no people. Anyway, I didn't think too much about it. I parked my car and looked for signs to the toilets. I didn't see any but in front of me were some double doors leading to the restaurant seating areas. Walking through I was again surprised to notice that there was no one there. At this point a man appeared from out of view carrying a tray full of food and drink. Never taking his eyes of me he sat down at a table facing me and continued to stare. I couldn't help thinking how unusual he looked and it made me feel a little uneasy. I looked away and tried to find signs for the toilets but there were none so I started to walk around the inside of the building, and still the place was empty except for this peculiar man and me. I began to wonder whether perhaps the toilets were outside so I walked back to the front doors. Now, as I am writing this I'm wondering whether the man was still there at this point because I don't think he was . . . anyway, when I reached the front doors I noticed two uniformed youths standing by a fast food counter, a boy and a girl. I approached the lad and asked him where the toilets were. "This way," he said and led me around the back of the fast food counter; still I could see no signs for the toilets. When I came out the boy and girl were still there, the man with the tray of food had certainly gone but still nobody else. I returned to my car, drove down the slope and back on to the hurly-burly of the main road.

I can recall thinking as I left just how very strange this experience had been. I have never, ever, come across a deserted service station on a busy road, not even at night (and this was lunchtime on a Friday). It was then that I noticed how peculiar I felt and this brought to mind a journey I had made to Long Sutton two years previously. On that occasion I had experienced two hours of missing time. Immediately I looked at the car's clock but it seemed in order and I didn't feel anywhere near as *mentally dislocated* as I had the time before:

A missing two hours

It was the 5th August 2004 and I had driven my friend, counsellor and *abduction* researcher, Mary Rodwell from Oxford to North Walsham in Norfolk where she was to catch up with family and friends before returning home to Australia. From there I had arranged to visit my friends, Paul and Ann Andrews in Long Sutton, Lincolnshire. [4]

We reached North Walsham at 3pm on Thursday 5th August. I stayed for a cuppa and a chat was given directions for the quickest route to Long Sutton and drove away at 3.30pm. I was told it would take just over an hour.

Mary Rodwell

As I motored towards the town of Thorpe Market I made a mental note to stop after I'd cleared Kings Lynn to phone and let Ann know when I would arrive and reminded myself that I must telephone my partner in Australia when I arrived.

The drive was smooth and uneventful - no hold-ups or delays. I was still some way from Kings Lynn on the A148 road when I happened upon a parking area and felt compelled to drive into it, which I did. The crescent-shaped parking area was hidden behind a row of trees and bushes and a medium-size white box-truck was already there. It had a name on the side that I recognised (but afterwards couldn't remember for a long time). I pulled up behind the truck, rang Ann and told her that I was about 10 miles the other side of Kings Lynn from her and would probably be about 40 minutes. (I gave myself extra time in case I met any delays - which was why I had originally planned to phone her AFTER Kings Lynn.) I hung up and drove back out to the road; as I did so an identical white truck (with the same name) was approaching from my right so I put my foot down and drove on towards Kings Lynn. Once on the highway I realised immediately that I felt somehow disorientated, groggy, queasy . . . and burnt. I put it down to the several hours of

---

[4] This all occurred on the ancient festival of 'Lughnasadh' - a time dedicated to the step-mother of the Celtic lightning hero 'Lugh', their 'St. Michael'.

driving I had done on this hot day, even though I had rested at North Walsham. I had been feeling perfectly ok when I drove into the parking place. A little down the road I noted a sign that said Kings Lynn 6 miles.

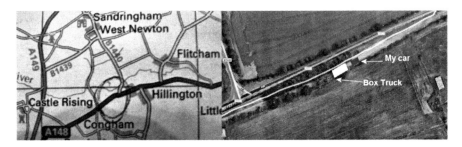

I later discovered that the parking area is only 2 or 3 miles from the royal palace of Sandringham and opposite the B1440, which leads to it. Is there a doorway through time near Sandringham? Was my experience somehow connected to this?

When I drove into Kings Lynn I came to a set of traffic lights and had to choose between two lanes: one to turn left and the other to carry straight on. I knew I needed to drive straight on but chose the lane to turn left. I felt extremely confused but did manage to see I was in the wrong lane before I got to the lights so I stopped, indicated to get into the correct lane and someone let me through. It was a little slow driving through the outskirts of Kings Lynn but nothing too tiresome. However I still felt very strange indeed.

Approaching Sutton Bridge I had the strange sensation, almost a mechanical feeling, of my consciousness clicking into another gear - it was like abruptly waking up but not fully. At this point I noticed two red, round signs with white bars across their middle, and one atop the other. I immediately recognised them as 'NO ENTRY' signs...and slammed  on my brakes - as did every other car behind me. They also (understandably) began to thrash at their horns and (no doubt) deliver streams of obscenities. Still not fully *with it* I could see a stream of cars crossing from the other side of the road in the other lane but nothing in front of me on my side. I was so confused. I didn't know whether I was barred from crossing the bridge but I reasoned that I must be able to because there was nowhere else to go even though the NO ENTRY signs clearly (to me) said I could not. I gingerly drove across. [5]

In less than 10 minutes I was at Ann's house and she was putting the kettle on. As she did so I remembered that I had to phone my partner so I asked Ann,

"What's the time, about 5 o'clock...?"

"No", she said, "It's 20 to 7!!"

I couldn't believe it; three hours to drive 70 miles! A journey I was told would take me about one hour!!

Ann said that she'd been worried: "I wondered where you got to. You telephoned me at 4.15. I thought you must have gone for a look around Kings Lynn or something." I still felt disorientated, queasy and hot. My coordination was hampered and I found everything very difficult to do but gradually during the evening I felt better and better. It wasn't until the next morning that I realised what I had risked - without any comprehension of the peril at the time.

Something happened to me at that lay-by I'm convinced of it. I lost approximately two hours somewhere. My fuel gauge (oddly) read the same the next morning as it did when I left North Walsham. Unfortunately I didn't take notice of the mileage but even my cars don't run on fresh air.

I tried and tried to remember the name on the side of the truck but it took another 22 months . . . and my recall came in a very strange, and slightly sinister, way. In May 2006, I was watching the TV drama, 'See No Evil' about the Moors Murders and in a street scene the white box truck appeared briefly. It was an exact match for the truck in that lay-by near Sandringham; even the name on the side: REPCO. I'd remembered at last! [6]

The reason why the name had been familiar to me was that it is the name of quite a well-known automotive firm in

---

[5] A couple of days later I drove over the bridge again and the "NO ENTRY" signs were not on top of each other (of course). They were on each side of the roads on the pillars.
[6] See No Evil: The Moors Murders (2006): www.imdb.com/title/tt0491807

Australia, where I used to live. Apart from on the truck in the television programme I haven't seen the name here in the UK. I think it's very odd and the nagging feeling that the REP part of the name on the truck in the lay-by might be short for REPTILIAN doesn't go away.

I have not yet got to the bottom of what happened in that secluded lay-by in August 2004, but let's get back to 2006 and I've just left the service station somewhere near Silver-stone:

On the road again

I estimated that the visit to the service station had taken me about 8 to 10 minutes – if that. As it transpired I did meet two traffic jams on the journey and it was a good job that I had stopped. After the second one I was following another vehicle along a brand new and straight bypass when a couple of cops flashed a speed gun at us but I never received a ticket. Other than these incidents the drive was uneventful and did not seem out of the ordinary in any way; except that I cannot remember much about the last stretch of the journey, the long, flat, straight as a die, road to Paul and Ann's house.

There are anomalies that I cannot account for, at least at the moment. One of them is to do with the time I arrived.

Arrival

My recollection is that I drove straight to Sutton Bridge post office to pay my road tax. This, according to my receipt, was at 4.46pm. Sutton Bridge is 5 minutes drive away from Paul and Ann's home. I remember the journey all the way from the post office to the crossroads near their house but after that is a mystery until I get out of my car, in pitch-darkness, at their house. I fumbled in the dark to find the bolt on the iron

Crossroads near the Andrews' home

gates, lifted it and cautiously inched my way across the lawn to the front door. I knocked and was relieved to see Ann's smiling face as she welcomed me in.

Ann showed me into their newly-built conservatory appended to the side of their spacious lounge where my good friends: fellow experiencer and author, Mike Oram and his lovely partner Fran, who is a great author, were engrossed in conversation with a lady, who I'd communicated with, but never met before, Paola Harris.

After greeting each other and being introduced to Paola I was told that Ann and Paul's son Jason, and Jacqui, his wife, were expected shortly and that they were picking up a person called Sacha from the train station.

Paola Harris

The reason for my visit, other than to catch up with my friends Ann, Paul, Jason and Jacqui Andrews and Mike and Fran, was to attend a talk that Paola, a renowned Italian/American journalist and UFO researcher, was to give on the Saturday night, in a village called Bergh Apton, for the Norfolk UFO Society, Sacha had been dispatched by UFO Data Magazine to report on the event and to interview Paola.[7]

I didn't question the circumstances at the time but it puzzled me during the next week how I had come to arrive in full-on darkness. It was the 29th September and the night doesn't fall until after 7pm at this time of year. It should have been no later than 5pm and so it should still have been light. Interesting too - and I think this might be significant - is that the dates of both the 2004 and 2006 road-*trips* have such strong links to the *Dragon-Slayer*, St. Michael. This journey occurred at *Michaelmas*, the feast day of St. Michael.

I telephoned Ann to see whether she could remember what time I had arrived and she said that she thought it was between 7 and 8pm and remembered that it was dark because she had to put the light on. Paul, both he and Ann told me, had asked why I hadn't parked in the drive and I had answered that it was because it was dark and that I had found it difficult to open the gates. Ann, Paul and Fran, when I asked them later, said that I seemed very tired, and slightly dishevelled upon arrival. I had also complained of feeling *out of sorts* and having a bad headache. Ann had made me a sandwich and a cup of tea and remembered that she had to switch on the table lamp too. Paul and Ann had assumed that I had

[7] www.ufodata.co.uk

driven down straight after finishing work and had had nothing to eat. (This seems to corroborate the late hour that it seems I had arrived.)

According to the AA the journey time should take 2 hours 33 minutes from my home to Long Sutton. I had left home at 12.30pm so there are about 1 ½ hours to be accounted for (the journey from my home to Sutton Bridge). There had, as I said before, been traffic jams along the route, two of them, and they were both quite long and tedious. I had stopped, once to visit a cash point in Wheatley (5 minutes max.) and then at the service station, but at that point, as I mentioned before there seemed to be no time anomaly, according to the car's clock. Another 10 minutes, say? So I must have been in the traffic delays for about 1 ¼ hours, or was I? And then how come there appears to be another 2 ¼ to 3 ¼ period of missing time if in fact I arrived at the Andrews at 7 or 8pm rather than 5 o'clock?

There is another twist. Still perplexed by my arriving at the Andrew's home in darkness and the seeming contradictions of it I telephoned Fran. She said that she was pretty sure that I had turned up somewhere between 7 and 8pm, but that she would check with Mike, which she did. Mike said that he *wanted to say* between 7 and 8pm but seemed to remember it was 5pm, because Paola had mentioned that a car had just arrived – mine. Fran said that she had deliberately not prompted Mike regarding the timing so why did Mike <u>want</u> to say between 7 and 8pm? I wrote to Paola and she emailed back:

About your arrival, It was at 5:00...but not dark...Not at all...and you saw a man in the rain...It was raining buckets.

I'd forgotten about the rain and I really don't think that I would have crept across the lawn if it had been light and *raining buckets*. I'd forgotten about the man too, but I remember now. It was a little while after I had arrived and I was looking out of the back window when I spotted a figure bolt across my view and through the gate into the chicken run. It was tipping with rain, chucking it down. I commented on it to the others and thought it was probably Paul going to lock the chooks up; but Ann said they hadn't got the chicken run anymore. In the morning I went to take a look but there weren't any footprints in the now very muddy ground either.
(I do remember from a previous visit that I had discovered an energy stream flowing by this particular location, which may well be connected to this sighting.

Jason, a friend of his, Jacqui and Ann told me about some very scary incidents that occurred late at night when Jason and Jacqui lived in a mobile home just the other side of the hedge from the chicken run. They were suffering continual harassment from a coven of Satanists who had been viciously attacking their horses, chanting at the house and had also burned the field just behind them. There had too been occasions of them hammering on the walls of the mobile home issuing threats and more chanting. One night a group of friends came to visit the two Js in their mobile home when without warning, and for no reason, one of the lads launched into a raging possessed fury. Fortunately Jason was more than equal to what was happening and was able to quell the threat.)

Jason's former bedroom - Notice the orbs in the corner. This is the portal where the beings come in. J told me this years ago.

Ann doesn't remember it raining when she opened the door to me either. Something is amiss and puzzling here. Was *Time* distorting, or somehow being manipulated? Someone (Paola) sitting in one part of the room was experiencing a radically different time and space perspective to other people (Ann and Fran) sitting just a few yards away, while someone else (Mike) who was sitting in between was unsure which reality he was experiencing. Of course this is all conjecture and the possibility exists that I did arrive at 5pm, that it was hissing down and that I was just tired from driving: but before you make up your mind read on . . .

Paola had been staying with Ann and Paul, sleeping in Jason's former bedroom, for the previous two nights but had decided to book a hotel room for the remaining two. Mike and Fran were staying too - after a last minute decision to attend Paola's talk as well as the preceding daytime *Mind, Body and Spirit Fair*. I had been expecting to sleep in Jason's room but arrangements had been altered because Mike and Fran were there. They took Ann and Paul's elder son, Daniel's former room, which meant that Paola was accommodated in Jason's.

For readers that are not aware of this, Jason Andrews, now 25-years-old has conscious recall of every one of his previous lives and has had

continuous experiences with *otherworldly* beings since before he was born (this time). Every member of his family has witnessed supernatural events, mostly to do with Jason; although previous to his birth it was Daniel alone who was attracting these entities, or so they thought. It has subsequently been discovered that Ann herself has a long, and sometimes very emotional, history too.

It seems to be incredibly difficult for some people to accept, until they meet them, that the Andrews' are just a very ordinary family, 'much like most others', as Ann would insist. I've known them for quite a few years now and I'll tell you what if you didn't know that their lives were filled with such bizarre experiences you would never guess. Even after all the media attention they have had there is not one iota of ego and no *airy-fairy* airs; down-to-earth is what they are. They are good, honest, hard-working people with the same bills and everyday concerns as everyone else but on top of this they've had to cope with always perplexing, sometimes frightening, intrusions from *otherworlds* - and our own military and government agencies.

As well, like me and many others who live with similar experiences, they have to somehow synthesise what their experiences show them is real with what orthodoxy insists is true. It isn't easy. They, like I do, find that the very best way to deal with these experiences as well as the pallid certainty of resolute sceptics and what I call, *Moloch's mouthpieces* is to see the funny side. To banish this dis-ease of the *Darkness* we laugh. Ann Andrews has written two great books: *Abducted, The True Story of Alien Abduction* (with Jean Ritchie) and *Walking Between Two Worlds ~ Belonging to None*) There is an online interview that Paola conducted with Jason on her website at www.paolaharris.it/jason.htm

Paola, who has interviewed many of the most well-informed people in secret technologies, ufology, conspiracy, psychic phenomena and remote-viewing, did not want to spend one more night in the farmhouse:

"I want to get some sleep! I have to give a presentation tomorrow," she pleaded.

During both nights she had been woken many times by doors creaking open and by footsteps walking up and down the stairs and along the landing; footsteps that belonged to no incarnate person! It was like Piccadilly Circus! Fran had heard them too. (On a previous occasion that Mike and Fran had stayed there this pacing about had happened. Mike had ventured out to investigate but found nobody, yet the footsteps continued.) During this latest visit, at one point their bedroom door opened and someone or something sat on the side of Fran's bed.

Paola's no *scaredy*-cat, the nature of her work means that she just cannot think that way. She just needed some sleep! Paola and I swapped books and I recommend her book, *Connecting the Dots* to everyone who is interested in what is really going on in our world. It is crammed full of fascinating interviews with such well-known people to alternative, and cutting-edge, research as Col. Philip Corso, Zecharia Sitchin, Dr. Michael Wolf, Dr. Steven Greer, Sgt. Clifford Stone, Sgt. Major Robert O. Dean, Richard Hoagland, Padre Corrado Balducci (Vatican), David Icke, Dr. Richard Sigismond, R. Leo Sprinkle, Clark McClelland (NASA), Alex Collier, Uri Geller, Ingo Swann, Paul Smith, Dr. Courtney Brown, Dr. Russell Targ, John Mack and more. I loved it.

Anyway . . . back in the conservatory, as we chatted and listened to Paola's absorbing stories of her friendships and meetings with so many intriguing characters, I was feeling extremely tired and hungry and my head was pounding. At this point I had no inkling of how long my journey had been and that it was so late. Ann, bless her, hurried off and brought me a plate of cheese sandwiches and a cup of tea and soon I was feeling much better. I still had a banging headache though, but I hoped the food would put paid to that. Shortly after this we all moved to the lounge and continued our chat when Jason, Jacqui and Sacha arrived. We had a really entertaining evening discussing all the interesting stuff we all experience and then, I think about midnight, we decided it was time for bed. Jason drove Paola to her hotel, Mike and Fran retired to Dan's former bedroom, Sacha to Jason's and me (what a gentlemen!) got the sofa. I remember whilst Ann was sorting out some blankets for me she asked whether I would prefer to sleep on the sofa in the conservatory "as it is much more comfortable". *Something* urged me not to.

It didn't register at the time but the sofa I was to *sleep* on is directly under Jason's bedroom.

A most terrible night

I lay down to sleep on the sofa and was just drifting off when the clock chimed loudly. 'I hope that it doesn't keep me awake all night,' I thought. Then immediately I heard this loud scratching noise coming from the back of the room, either the patio doors or the back window. 'Oh, go away!' I grumbled to myself, 'I'm not up for this tonight, I'm too tired.' The next thing, directly behind me, I could hear several objects moving about on the coffee table, scraping along the surface and through my closed eyelids I saw bright lights flashing around the room. Next came some garbled voices . . . what they were saying I could not comprehend. Then quick as a flash something shot right into my head, it felt like my brain was being squeezed, and it bloody well hurt! By this time I felt paralysed and could not move and I had the sense that whatever this was it was trying to read my mind. I saw visions . . . A great long bridge that spanned a bay, which could have been the Golden Gate Bridge in San Francisco, although after looking at photos of this, it was much longer than that. I think it was symbolic. Right now I cannot remember what the other visions were but what came next left me with proof that what was happening was very real.

Somehow I got to be standing at Ann's back door. I was looking out towards the sheds but it was pitch black, darker than hell. Then I noticed something moving around my feet; and it rose up. It was a large black dog, with eyes that looked back to before the dawn of everywhere; and flecks of white on it. The beast began to chew on the ends of the fingers on my right hand; not biting chewing, and hard. I felt the dampness and the breath and I couldn't move or call out. From behind this dog came another big black dog which also rose up. The first dog nudged the second away and then resumed its  chewing . . . and then the clock chimed, and there was daylight. It seemed to me as if I had only just gone to bed. I got up and climbed the stairs to the bathroom. As I did so I passed Jason's bedroom and saw that the door was open. Sacha was awake and dressed sorting the bedclothes out. 'I've had the most terrible night!' she trembled. Not wanting to awaken anyone else I suggested that we go down stairs, have a cup of tea, and then she could tell me about it.

"I heard these voices talking to each other," she said shaking, "And I couldn't move, but I could see that I was wrapped in something like cling-film, and I was hot and sweating. "I brought this tape recorder along with me and I left it on. It starts recording when it hears something. . . and listen to this. . ."

She switched it on and peculiar sounds emanated from the device. There were more things that occurred but I'll leave that for Sacha to relate.

Afterwards I began to tell her what had happened to me.

"And then there was this dog . . . ' I said

. . ."*The dogs, oh no, the dogs!"* she cried, *"They were biting the top of my hand. . .look they've left bruises on it."* Then she paused, seeming to be confused, *"They were biting my other hand, this one! How can that happen?"* On Sacha's hand were several small dark reddish-brown bruises. Several weeks later they were still there!

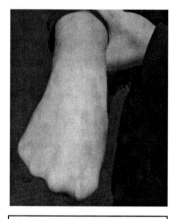

The bruises left on Sacha's hand by the hounds.

I had no bruises on my own fingertips that could be seen but the first joints felt very tender, and did for weeks afterwards. The skin was very sore to touch – as if they were severely sunburnt. My hair fell out in clumps and my facial hair did not grow for nearly a week - which was a bonus! For a long time, weeks, I did not feel myself. It was as if my mind had been split and hadn't been put together again properly. Things I could easily do with my eyes shut I found difficult. I was forgetting simple things, and more concerning, I seemed to be a different person in some ways. I found myself saying things that I didn't agree with. My friends started to notice these discrepancies. I think this has been much the same for Sacha.

Before I had arrived at Ann's house, I think it had been on the Wednesday, Paola took some photographs of Jason's bedroom and also of the landing, two of which she has very kindly allowed me to reproduce here. It appears that the whole of Jason's bedroom is shuddering - is it between worlds? - and there is something very strange going on with the landing too, as you can see. Paola tells me that she showed the photographs to Pascal Riolo a noted Belgium Psychic. He said that the family is part of an experiment being conducted by several groups of aliens. On the Thursday Ann took a video of Jason's room (which she showed me later) where a bedside light seems to be fading in and out of substance.

I was standing in the garden chatting with Mike on the Saturday morning when I spotted a seagull flying over. As it reached a point maybe 70 yards behind the house it suddenly crashed into something invisible, seemed to reverse, rallied itself, and then flew around whatever the unseen barrier was.

Paola's talk was outstanding (she was as well surrounded by orbs throughout, some of which I saw and photographed). The Saturday night went off without any more incidents.

I drove home on the Sunday afternoon and made much better time arriving in just over 2 ½ hours. I didn't notice anything missing from my home but an internal door was open even though I'd made a point of shutting it.

The following week saw the now usual late night phone calls with no one answering on the other end.

On the Friday I was preparing for my trip to St Anne's in Lancashire to speak at the PROBE conference, opened my sock drawer and right there was the piece of

Paola Harris (and orbs) speaking at Burgh Apton, Norfolk.

palisander wood that Inti Caesar had given me; which had been missing since 26th April 2006.

Healing

Another conference I attended soon after the disturbing events at Ann Andrew's house in the early hours of 30th September 2006 was Andrew Collins' *QuestCon* conference in London. It was something that my friend Paul said to me there that sort of inspired this book:

We were chatting over lunch when he suddenly enquired, *"Are you ok Ellis?"* I knew that I wasn't, and hadn't been myself since the service station incident on my way to South Lincolnshire. That someone else noticed, and was concerned enough to ask, was touching and I knew that I had to do something. I don't know why I didn't think of it before. Perhaps I needed the trigger that Paul gave me and that enabled me to reconnect. On the train journey home I knew exactly what to do. All I needed was to ask for healing, which I did and immediately I was beginning to feel better.

A few days later I was relating the events at the Andrews' to my friend Geoff Ambler, who is vice-president of the long established Contact International UFO Research Group. Geoff is a dowser, as well as a researcher into all things supernatural. After I left he dowsed my energy signature and was concerned that I had 'picked up' some negative presence.

The following Wednesday (8th November) at a Contact International Group meeting he dowsed my energy field and discovered two *spiritual* attachments, one either side of me. When I looked around to watch his pendulum it would stop and if I closed my eyes it would stop spinning too. He felt that these were harmful presences and decided he should remove them. I was less certain because I know that I have two guardians. They are reptilians, dragons then, fully armoured. I was concerned that what he was going to do would in some way hamper them. Geoff said he had done the deed.

The next night (Thursday) I was awoken by scratching, the same scratching I had heard at Paul and Ann's while sleeping on their sofa. I'd tried to move but couldn't and no matter how hard I tried to I could not call out. It seemed the longest time that I was like this and then eventually I managed to cry out and immediately I could move again. My *spacey-ness* returned, though not as drastically as before, and I spent the next day in a sort of haze. On the Friday night I was well enough again to remember what I should do and asked for healing and my protection to return. Come Saturday morning I was feeling great. I called in to see Geoff on the Sunday and he dowsed me again saying that he could pick up nothing negative but remembering a previous experience he said he would like to dowse my car. As soon as he reached his pendulum into the car it span like mad. He performed his stuff on it and the pendulum's lack of movement confirmed to him that all was now well.

I didn't tell him about this but on my way to visit him I had dropped by to visit another friend. They live on a hill close to St Mary's Church in Garsington, Oxfordshire.[8]

Their drive is steep so I engaged the handbrake as well as put the car in 1st gear when I parked. When I arrived my friend was in their driveway. We had been chatting for about 5 minutes when I saw a car speed past up the hill towards the centre of the village, just at that moment my car whizzed quickly down the slope and crashed into the bank on the other side of the road. I ran down after it and found the handbrake had been released and the gears stick in neutral. This could have ended tragically but fortunately no people or other vehicles came by at that moment. My car has only recently been tested (MOT) and has behaved properly ever since. It makes me wonder, "Did Geoff's pendulum truly pick up something sinister?"

Shadow Walking

About 3 years ago, perhaps more, I dreamed a journey. It began near two old thatched cottages along an old dirt farm track:

I ambled along, but with a purpose that was unknown to me at the time. Following my shadow, etched by the hot sun, I turned sharp right to follow a road that is there now, but not then.

It took a while to realise that I was 'dream travelling'. As I walked, the scene and my presence, including my dress, flickered in and out of different eras. I saw no one. Presently I crossed a farmyard and made for a hill in the distance. I recognised it: Toot Baldon Hill.

I crossed fields of long dry grass and thirsty streams and in a while I reached an oak tree. Here I had to dig. Something of immense

---

[8] www.ellisctaylor.com/inthemarianfields.html

significance was buried here long ago by the inhabitants of a village during a time of great peril - Saxons have something to do with it, but the story begins well before they ever set foot in Albion and it is connected with invading forces. I thought to myself, *I know this tree.*

I have related this true story to a few friends and I have always intended to have a poke around that tree; but alas, the tree has died and the farmer has removed it now but, although I haven't seen for myself, the stump, or its roots remain. How do I know?

Well, I was at a gathering of friends and one of them pulled out a photograph that Andrew King had taken of the 7th July 2007 crop formation at Toot Baldon. Another friend, who is a *recovering* metal *detectorer* (or whatever they call them) piped up, *"Never mind the crop circle I can't take my eyes of the crop marks!"* - The *ghosts* of what look like some large buildings and enclosures are very prominent in the photo and what's more, they surround the remains of the old tree, which happens to be on the St. Michael Line (See my article, *The St Michael Line from Marsh Baldon to Garsington.* (X on the map page 27.)

In late 2006 I came across an old photograph in a book. The photo shows what look like the two thatched cottages from my *dream-journey*. The cottages are long gone but the book says that a family that lived in one of the cottages was called 'Taylor'!

Is there really a treasure buried in this green field below St. Mary's church? Or are the ghostly crop marks the treasure? Whichever, something lays hidden here that is rare and valuable. Yet, this isn't the greatest treasure, there is more to the story; but this is the beginning . . . and I hope to uncover it all one day . . . and write about it.

I telephoned the offices of Oxford Archaeology and told them about the crop marks and gave them the website addresses of the Oxford

Centre for Crop Circle Studies and the Crop Circle Connector; unsurprisingly I have heard nothing back from them. [9]

At about the same time that the Toot Baldon crop circle was being formed my friend Winston Keech was sitting it out, wide awake - with two companions and his dog - on Knapp Hill overlooking the famous crop circle target, East Field, near Alton Barnes in Wiltshire. Armed to the teeth with the latest in camera technology Win has sat out in all weathers for the past 10 years or so ever since he witnessed a ball of light seeming to produce a crop circle. What he managed to capture on film this night is extraordinary - a crop circle just laying itself out in the field in about 15 seconds. Win is an exceptionally kind man with infinite integrity and he was kind enough show me his film. Win says he doesn't persist in his quest for money or glory and I believe him. He wants to show his film to the world but it isn't as easy as some people might think - for all sorts of reasons.

Another very famous and rightly so, crop circle event happened on this date (7th July) too, at Stonehenge; this time in 1996. The circle design was a 'Julia Set' mathematical fractal - which matches the date - think about it - Julia = July and Set = sept = 7. The date was also the very magical 777 - just like Toot and East Field. The number combination describes a divine message or messenger - an angel's whisper - one that is only noticed by those who are alert to notice it. A very few sadly.

I visited Stonehenge in 1997. This ancient and awe-inspiring temple of stones is presided over by the National Trust who use this site to fund many of its other *possessions*. In keeping with *Darkness* practices it has constructed a path around the monument that ushers visitors to walk around the stones anti-clockwise. When I arrived there were hundreds of visitors all obediently following the line. So, I set off in the opposite direction (clock-wise) accompanied by *tut-tuts* and glaring stares, not that it bothered me. After a few yards I stopped near the ropes and as I silently wondered at the enormity and significance this place must have had to its builders a lady guide approached me:

"I noticed that you know what you are doing," she said.

Awoken from my musing I stared blankly at her.

[9] http://contactinternationalufo.homestead.com/cropcircles.html
www.cropcircleconnector.com/2007/tootbalden/tootbalden2007.html

"You are following the correct direction, the natural flow at this site," she added.

I said something but she quickly asked, "Have you ever stood on the Aubrey Holes?" I told her I hadn't. "Come with me," she said. We walked clockwise around the stones to the other side and she pointed out a circular piece of white *concrete.*

"Stand on there," she said.

As soon as I did a wave of tingling energy rushed up through my body and I felt like my hair was standing on end.

"You can feel it, can't you," she gleefully offered. *"We stand on them in the winter to keep us warm."*

We chatted for a while. I asked her which field the beautiful *Julia Set* crop circle was in the year before. She pointed the field out and said, *"Do you know, it just appeared from nowhere. Everyone was milling about just like today and one minute it was just a plain field and the next there it was. I'll never forget it. I always think of it as a very special gift for me. You see my name's Julia!"*

The 'Julia Set' crop circle is one of the outstanding mysteries of crop circle research. On the same day it appeared a pilot flew over the field on his way to somewhere else. He reports that there was definitely no formation in it. Less than an hour later his passenger driving past the field noticed a crowd of people. When he got out to investigate there it was. This crop formation had something like 151 circles in it and was over 900 feet from nose to tail. 151 adds to 7.

A green hill far away

In June of 1997, on the 24th it was, I went to visit an acquaintance, who is a laser scientist, in Stadhampton, a village across the river from Chislehampton in Oxfordshire. He'd not long been in his ancient, tiny but three-storey stone cottage and he was keen to show me around. "We'll start at the top. There's a brilliant view from there," he said eagerly beckoning me to lead the way up the steep and narrow little staircase.

"Don't mind the mess," he said, "I've piled all the stuff in there that I haven't sorted out yet."

When I reached the third floor there were some boxes in the way of the window so I shifted them over and as I stood up I could see right across to Chislehampton - and there, right on the side of a hill, and looking magnificent, was a crop circle! "There's a crop circle!" I blurted out. It was the first time I'd ever seen one in the field. "Where?" shouts Andy scrambling for a squizz out of the window. "So it is!" I'll have to go and look at it later. That was the second strange thing Andy had encountered in my company (See 'Blue light' page 67). His scientific dog was in danger of walking - good job he's got an open mind.

Not long prior to this I'd made the acquaintance of Geoff Ambler who was the president of the Oxford – based, Contact International UFO Research Group. (The group incidentally, that the late Graham Birdsall, much-missed editor of the very success*ful UFO Magazi*ne, began his UFO career with.) Geoff is also a keen crop circle enthusiast and is very involved with the Oxfordshire Centre for Crop Circle Studies (OCCCS). When I got back to where I was staying (I was on holiday from Australia) I rang Geoff expecting him to already know about the crop circle. He didn't, and no one else had reported it either. Geoff and I arranged to meet up later that day to visit the formation in order to survey and photograph it - which we did, after gaining the farmer's permission to go into his crop. He was very helpful. A nice guy; he reckoned he knew who had made it – some local *likely lads* on the way home from the pub, he reckoned.

The ground was very muddy, sticky, and the crop was wet and blown every-which-way. The weather had been horribly windy and wet for several days and nights. At the time I knew *sweet FA* about crop circles and, as I said, this was to be my very first time inside one. I was excited, not knowing what to expect. I'd heard that some people could hear strange sounds inside them. Others reported severe headaches; occasionally it was the very opposite; they were healed, they said.

It was impossible to get to the formation without traipsing through thick and claggey wet clay soil and by the time we arrived we were both 6 inches taller than when we started. I wondered why there weren't any great sods of mud on the wheat (besides us) if this was a prank by some local *blathered* yahoos - like the farmer had suggested to us. Another thing that puzzled me as we walked in was that none of the stems of wheat were damaged or broken as far as I could see.

Geoff had brought his circle-surveying gear – a long tape measure, a camera, pen and paper, and his pendulum. We set to and began measuring out the circles. There were 5 of them. One large central circle surrounded by four smaller ones. Geoff said this design was known as a 'Celtic Cross', 'a rather *old-fashioned* type,' he said mournfully. My heart sank a little because it might have been run-of-the-mill to him but it was *magical* to me.

Richmond Hill crop formation
24th June 1997 G. Ambler

But he didn't mean it the way I took it. I can't say that I felt anything but grace and wonder in that formation. How, for instance, did they manage to get from circle to circle without damaging the wheat. It was one heck of a jump. 'Perhaps they pole-vaulted,' I mused - No footprints or scuffs on the clay, no lumps of mud on the pristine wheat, no holes in the centres of the circles, no damaged stems and . . . the circles were not circles. They were *expertly* shaped and positioned, so that when viewed from the air the impressions in the green wheat, on this curvy hillside, looked perfectly round.

Chislehampton church and manor house
(Chislehampton House) from Richmond Hill

How do drunks, in the hissing rain and howling wind, in the middle of the night, an arrow's flight from the farmhouse, and the sinister, 'Tiny' Rowland's 'Chislehampton House' (you read that right) construct such confounding magnificent geometry – and why? I considered that perhaps a swirling energy force had been exerted either from above or below. Perhaps that would account for the astonishing projected symmetry.

The crop circle was located in a field on what is now known as Richmond Hill but a 17th century map calls it 'Standing Hill'. I'm pretty sure that this field has been left to pasture ever since.

Even though I love this little corner of Oxfordshire the hill has a very peculiar energy and I don't like it. There's a sense of something foreboding and militaristic about it and it hasn't escaped my notice that the cross-like formation on a green hill appeared on St John's Eve.

Rumble in the jungle

The hills from Garsington church

Pagan activity in the woods

Wittenham woods from Sinodun Hill

Well . . . not quite, but several years ago, I can't quite remember when, but it was a Sunday, I decided to go for a walk on *Wittenham Clumps*, the *deux sein* hills above Long Wittenham and the abbey town of Dorchester-on-Thames, in Oxfordshire. The two peaks are quite a landmark in the area and on top of one of them (Sinodun Hill) the St. Michael and St. Mary ley lines cross. Below are woods where pagan rites are frequently held, and the River Thames threads through ancient meadows fair scattered with remnants of barrows and other earthworks. Where a lake now mirrors the sky and carp anglers snooze through the day there once stood a magnificent stone circle that rivalled and perhaps bettered Stonehenge.

As I walked around Sinodun Hill I came across a large paw print in the drying mud; it appeared to be too big for a dog and no imprints of claws were evident. I kicked myself for not having a camera with me, looked around to see if I could find any more - I couldn't - and made my way down across the meadow to the beech woods below. Except for a couple up near *the Poem Tree* on Sinodun I hadn't seen a soul.[10] Near the dew pond I swung through the farm gate and walked along the track and into the woods. I'd only got a few yards when from my left I heard something that made the hairs on the back of my neck stand on end - a low rumble that I recognised immediately, one that only a big cat makes . . . and it was coming from somewhere in the thick scrub only a matter of yards away. I stopped. Was I hearing things? And waited. A second or two later, no more, and the deep bellied rumble came again! It came . . . and I went . . . pretty smartish!

That evening I emailed a friend who lives quite close to Wittenham and told him about it. Although he is very interested in the paranormal, Forteana, UFOs and stuff he is also pretty sceptical. I think he suspected that I'd heard a muntjac deer (they kind of bark and there are lots of them in the woods) but I've heard muntjac bark scores of times and I've also heard big cats!

Not long after this my friend wrote to me. He said that he couldn't sleep one night so he had driven to the top of Sinodun Hill to gaze at the stars and perhaps spot a UFO. He left his car in the car park and walked up the hill to find a good spot overlooking the valley. He hadn't been there long when he heard a big cat roar from the woods below on his left. This was followed almost immediately by a second roar from his right. He decided that he didn't want to gaze at the sky after all and hurried back to his car. As he drove down the narrow lane towards the road a big cat ran right in front of him - very close by to where I had seen the paw print.

Ghost dogs

A few years ago, in Oxfordshire, I was driving from Wheatley to Garsington; it was mizzling and quite dark and I was last in a line of three cars. From the right, where there is a large field, a large black dog bounded fluidly across the road between my car and the one in front, and melted into the hedge. Time seemed to slow down. There was no way a real dog would have made it across the road with out being hit and the hedge here is so thick and thorny I can't see how this large

---

[10] The Poem Tree: A now dead, but still standing, beech tree carved with a poem Joseph Tubb of Warborough Green in 1844-5 www.berkshirehistory.com/odds/poem_tree.html

animal could possibly get through it. I remembered the spot and went back there the next day. There was no sign at all that anything had broken through the hedge and there were no tracks in the long grass and stinging nettles that grow on the road verge there. I later discovered that my friend Geoff Ambler had tracked the St Mary ley line through this precise spot.

My brother had a similar encounter with a large black dog while he was walking his own dog near Wheatley, in the twilight. The beast ran across the farm track and seemed to run straight through the fence. His dog took no notice, or didn't see it and he could find no tracks in the long grass either.

Craik's in time

On 22nd September 2007 I spoke at the Fourth Irish UFO Society Conference in the delightful town of Carrick-on-Shannon. (I also stayed in rooms numbered four and 301 in two hotels - number four is eternally present in my life. I write in depth about this number in my book, 'In These Signs Conquer'. The attraction of number four continues.)[11]

The day after the conference, organiser, and president of the Irish UFO Society, the amazing Betty Meyler (does anyone in Ireland not know Betty?) took a us out for a trip to Carrowmore, an astonishingly crowded mystical landscape on the Knocknarea Peninsular in County Sligo. In one stone circle, overlooked by the 'Cairn of Queen Maeve', high on the hill of Knocknarea, I felt impelled to stretch my arms, stand on my left leg and spin clockwise. It took no effort and I felt a surge of energy from the ground through me and out into the atmosphere. I shed a tear; there was something about this place that felt like home. [12]

When I told Betty that I was heading for Monaghan after the conference to visit a long time friend she suggested that I visit Castle Leslie, in Glaslough. 'Castle Leslie' is the ancestral home of the legendary UFO writer and investigator, spitfire pilot and celebrated *biffer* of Bernard Levin, the late Desmond Leslie. [13]

---

[11] www.ufosocietyireland.com/conference.htm
[12] www.megalithic.co.uk/article.php?sid=90
www.shee-eire.com/magic&mythology/Kings&Queens/Celtic/Queens/Connaught/Medb/Page1.htm
[13] A family historian writes regarding Desmond Leslie's prowess as a spitfire pilot during WW2:
"He destroyed a number of aircraft, most of which he was piloting at the time."
For more on Desmond Leslie please visit:
http://findarticles.com/p/articles/mi_qn4158/is_20010310/ai_n14377784

My friend had recently moved to Monaghan from Bantry Bay but I had no idea where in the county he had moved to. He'd moved to Glaslough!

While staying with my friend I visited the little church of St Salvators, just inside the castle grounds. As I wandered around the churchyard I saw a man with light, straight hair and wearing a grey cardigan about 50 yards in front of me. He looked over at me and then just faded away. I tried to take a photograph after this but the batteries had, well, given up the ghost!

On the way to Glaslough I took a bus to pay my respects to my ancestors at the portals of Knowth and Newgrange. While I was standing near the gateway to Newgrange I heard a young girl happily giggling as loud as can be from the other side of a wall but I couldn't see how anyone could be behind it, and me not see them, so I looked over; there was no girl there, nobody was there.

I'll tell you who was at Newgrange though; Minister of State and Teachta Dála (Assembly Delegate), Noel Ahern, the brother of the then embattled, now ex-Taoiseach (Prime Minister) Bertie Ahern. (It's a political dynasty.) I caught him emerging with his *off-siders* from the Newgrange portal and later speaking to young school kids. Appropriately-named Noel, was there to draw the names (energy) of a world-wide competition (search) for the right people to experience the Midwinter sunrise inside

Minister of State, Noel Ahern emerges from Newgrange.

the *time machine* on the 40th anniversary of the discovery of the Yule eye-light (sun-shaft) by Professor John O'Kelly. [14]

It was 28th September - 3 months before Noel's 63rd birthday (28th December) and an extremely active and potent ritual date; a date when rents and dues must be made ready and paid the next day. It was the 29th anniversary of Pope John Paul 1st murder, and also anniversaries of the 'Battle of the Clans', the Norman Invasion in Kent, the first public airing of the English National dirge, and in recent times - 22 years after the Pope's *offing* - this ignition date was used by Ariel Sharon too when he toured Temple Mount to provoke the Palestinians - all related in some way to islands (eye-lands) as well; but anyway the winners' energy was securely in the cauldron for Michaelmas.

SkyBow

On the 12th November 2007 I was walking near Oxford Castle with my friend Mac when I looked up in the sky and saw something that I'd never seen before - an upside-down rainbow just hanging in the sky above me. [15]

The Kirkstone Pass Inn

In the late 90s, on holiday from Australia I toured the Lake District of Angel-land (England). One day someone suggested that I visit 'the highest pub in England', the Kirkstone Pass Inn. It turned out not to be the highest but the third highest.

[14] www.independent.ie/national-news/fifty-lucky-winners-get-tickets-for-solstice-at-newgrange-1092163.html
www.knowth.com
www.irishmegaliths.org.uk
[15] The SkyBow: (a Circumzenithal arc) www.ellisctaylor.com/skybow.html

Anyway, I drove up the mountain pass to the ancient inn 1479 feet above sea level, parked up and walked across the lonely road to the front door. Pressing down the latch I was astonished to see a busy raucous tooth-challenged crowd of shabby revellers, some dressed in heavy coats, tricorn hats and grubby head-kerchiefs clutching tankards of ale around a large oak table . . . and then in a second the scene returned to a quiet rustic inn with a bar at the back and to the right.

I walked up to the bar and ordered a drink from the barman and asked him whether he knew the place was haunted. *'Oh yes'*, says he. If you look over there on the wall you'll see lots of letters and magazine articles describing what people have seen here over the years.

Leaving my drink on the bar I climbed the back stairs to the toilets. I had only just got in there when I heard something like a coin, or a marble, drop onto the tile floor and roll around. I looked all over the floor but there was nothing there. When I returned to the bar I wandered over to read through the reports and then sat down. I had a video camera with me and briefly scanned the pub. When we reviewed the film later a spine-chilling groan has been recorded.

On another occasion I was upstairs in the small hallway when the door next to me slammed loudly - but the door was already shut.

I've since captured masses of orbs in the Kirkstone. On one visit a group of people were sitting by the stairs when their little Jack Russell terrier got up and started growling and carrying on at something on the stairs. Figuring it was time to leave the group got up and left the pub. Taking my camera out of my bag I took a photograph of the location they were in. There are orbs all over the place . . . including one with a cat's face inside it - on the stairs! [16]

---

[16] The Kirkstone Pass Inn www.kirkstonepassinn.com

Past lives

It was a warm summer's evening and I was visiting a friend for a psychic circle in a seaside suburb of Perth. I was early but I sat down and closed my eyes.

Immediately I was walking along a bustling street in London. Horses trotted backwards and forwards pulling loads of coal, greengroceries and other wares past pedestrians, little stalls and huddles of people. The streets were dirty and the air smelled of coal and cabbages. Above the melee a newspaper vendor was calling out that the Lusitania had been sunk. I was a student, a poor one by the looks of it, my shoes had holes in them and were badly scuffed; I was dressed in worn clothes, a white shirt and dark, patched jacket and trousers. I walked through a grimy brick arch under a bridge and into what seemed almost another world. Although I could still hear the commotion on the other side of the bridge, it became more muffled. Here the streets were quiet. Long terraces of smart brick houses lined the road, each with their own iron railings and steps up to their front doors. I crossed the road to one of these houses, stopped, looked around, climbed the steps and pulled the brass door bell . . . g-dong! g-dong! The door was opened by a grey-haired lady in her late middle age wearing a long black dress. I introduced myself and she showed me into the Drawing Room.

Soon the door opened and a tall dark-haired man with a moustache came into the room. We spoke briefly and then I reached inside my jacket and pulled out some documents which I gave to the man. Patting my left shoulder with his right hand he thanked me and praised my courage for bringing the documents before escorting me to the front door. Before descending the steps into the street I pulled up my jacket collar quickly glanced around and hurried back to the busy streets on the other side of the arch. I felt cold.

I must have died shortly after this because during the latter years of World War II I was a blond woman in Tanganyika in Africa. I watched myself jump onto a jeep-like vehicle driven by a man in a British khaki uniform and drive away. We were involved in something that had to do with minerals.

Again I must have died shortly after this because within a decade I was born again, this time in Australia.

I'd been in Australia in a life before this. During the early days of British colonisation of Western Australia I was a young priest:

Standing next to a young novice and a severe old misery (the spitting image of Donald Rumsfeld with round spectacles) I was thoroughly enjoying watching a native Australian dance ceremony; so too was the young man but it was obvious that the elder priest detested it. All three of us were dressed in the black cassocks and saturno hats of the day. Suddenly all hell broke loose as at least a dozen troopers on horseback thundered into the arena shooting indiscriminately at the panicking people. One trooper ran down a young aboriginal girl and she fell. Just as he was about to launch his horse onto her I rushed out and grabbed his horse's reins . . . then everything went black. He'd brought his rifle butt down on my head!

One morning, in Australia early 1997, I awoke with a striking replay of a past life I had nine centuries previous to my Australian priest. I was a young soldier stumbling through a wood half dead, with terrible wounds and covered in blood when I came across a farmyard. I crawled into the yard and collapsed.

I don't know how long I lay there but it couldn't have been long. I came to with the motion of being dragged along the ground. My vision was clouded and my eyes stung but I could see that I was in a timber building. The ground was strewn with hay or straw and I could see through the walls to the outside. I realised I was in a barn. I felt something soft and wet touch my face. A girl, a young woman, dark-haired and dressed in an oatmeal coloured wide-sleeved dress was kneeling to my right-hand side gently bathing my wounds. I drifted in and out. I was suddenly roused by the clamour of thundering hooves and clashing metal, rough voices were balling out. I saw my nurse running out of the barn and into the yard where about 9 soldiers dressed in chainmail and Norman helmets reeled impatiently on their horses. One soldier was demanding to know if she had seen a stranger. The girl was saying that she hadn't. As this went on the other soldiers began riding around her the circle getting smaller and smaller until they were trampling her; she was screaming and I tried to get up but I couldn't . . . my right leg was strapped to a piece of heavy wood and my right arm too. It was then that an old man dressed in black, with long grey hair and beard hurried out. He held a long staff and he was crying out. Two or three of the soldiers broke away from the others and cut the old Jewish man down. I was sure that now the soldiers would come looking for me but they didn't . . . for some reason, after what sounded like a violent argument, they all rode off.

That is all I saw but I do know that I recovered and I avenged that old man and his daughter. That girl is now my partner.

Later that year, in England, I met up with an old friend who was going through a tough time. He needed a break from the toxic environment he was in and as I was going on a trip around sacred places in Wiltshire and Somerset he came along.

We were driving towards Stonehenge when I spotted two hitchhikers and stopped to offer them a lift. They were two friends, a male and a female who had just decided to go away for the weekend. They asked where we were going and when I told them they asked whether they could come with us. We had a brilliant time and I'll never forget it. I asked them if there was anywhere in particular that they would like to go and they said other than the places we were already heading for they would really like to visit a pub in Priddy, a small village in Somerset - because it had a great reputation for 'real ale'. I'd never heard of the place but I felt a strong urge to go there.

As soon as we drove into the village, and I saw the barn, the scene changed to my past life as a wounded soldier rescued by a young Jewish girl. As I write this the goose bumps I had then, when my eyes fell upon this enchanted little place, have returned and to think that I only went to Priddy because I picked up those two new-age travellers. I've always been so glad that I did.

I've since discovered that Priddy is reputed to have been visited by Jesus and that the visionary sacred song by William Blake and Charles Parry, 'Jerusalem' was based on this. [17]

I had lost the photo above but it came to light while I was writing this book. My partner had never seen it, nor ever been to Priddy. With no hint whatsoever I asked her if she recognised the place. *"That's where I lived when I was a Jewess,"* she responded without pause.

---

[17] Please see my book, IN THESE SIGNS CONQUER page 276

Underworld entrance

I mentioned in 'About the Author' that when I first lived in Oxford we had lived a stone's throw from the Radcliffe Observatory and was christened in St. Giles church.

I was four when I was taken with my sisters to be christened and I remember it like it was yesterday. I sat with my mum and dad and sisters in a line on the pew feeling a little nervous, not understanding what was going to happen. My dad said not to worry and that when it was over I could have a fruit pastille. Now most kids, if they remember their christening, will recall the minister pouring a little water from the font onto their forehead or perhaps they dipped their fingers in the font and made the sign of the cross on their forehead - that's what I've always seen anyway - but not me! I remember my head being full on pushed under the water in the font, I couldn't breath but my dad kept his promise.

A few years ago I went into St Giles church for the first time since those days and I noticed that the ancient carved stone font had been moved. The church that dates from 1120 was open because the world-famous St. Giles Fair was on. The vicar and a verger were in attendance and I mentioned that I'd been christened in the church but that the font wasn't in the spot where it is now. The vicar was impressed with my memory and confirmed that indeed the font had been relocated since then. [18]

In 2008 it was announced that a massive 5,000-year-old henge encircled by a deep moat had been discovered next to St Giles church during excavations for a new quadrangle for St. John's College. The presence of the henge, although said to be a 'new' discovery is clearly not. I have done a fair amount of work surveying the numerous potent and dormant leys (sacred alignments) that are linked to this site. [19]

---

[18] St. Giles church: www.sacred-destinations.com/england/oxford-st-giles-church.htm
    St. Giles: www.headington.org.uk/oxon/stgiles/fair/index.htm
[19] Oxford Henge: http://oxfordtalks.homestead.com/wow.html

I used to pass the observatory every Sunday morning when my parents or grandparents took me to Sunday school in an annexe of St. Giles Church. I remember one morning being taken to one of the cottages that backed on to the observatory and standing at the front door with, I think it was my Nan, while an elderly man - well, he seemed elderly to me then but he may not have been, I was only four-years-old at the most - talked to and

Excavation work for the new St John's College quadrangle. Remnants of the 'Oxford Henge' were discovered here.

about me. There is something very mysterious about this to me because otherwise it is such a vivid memory. I have always remembered this incident for some reason. The house was in Observatory Street, a few doors from the Woodstock Road. A little while ago I went back there to have a look at the area and immediately felt nauseous; memories of feeling intensely sick flooded back to me.

I don't ever recall it happening when we walked past there when I was a kid but every single time we drove past after going somewhere my head would *spin* (not literally - that would be something!), my eyes would haze over and I'd want to throw up. I'd get visions of paisley-like patterns and to this day I can't look at paisley patterns without feeling sick - yet for all this it still holds a fascination for me. What's that about! In recent times I have so

It was near to this gateway in Observatory Street that I met the man.

noticed how the pattern resembles a 2D section of DNA and also the mathematical fractal called a 'Julia Set', which relates very much to another mystery that I have already written about in my previous book, *In These Signs Conquer* but will mention again later.

Right where Observatory Street and the Woodstock Road meet there are some apartments and a huddle of shops known as Belsyre Court - the

Home Guard were stationed here during the war. Strangely enough 'Belsyre' means 'Godfather'.

Alexander Belsyre was a canon of Christ Church and the first president of St. Johns College - that owns most of the land around this part of Oxford. St. John the Baptist is the patron saint of tailors! It is all very weird and getting stranger . . .

The *Maltese Cross* topped observatory, which once adjoined and belonged to, the renowned Radcliffe Infirmary, (famed for its medical research too), now belongs to Templeton Green College, which was founded by Bury born geophysicist Cecil Howard Green and his wife Ida. It is claimed that Green, who was a founder of Texas Instruments, initially made his fortune through developing machines that could sense subsurface anomalies; which seeing as the observatory sits on an entrance to the Underworld is somewhat intriguing I think.[20]

Gurkha security
Radcliffe Infirmary site

Stone circle
John Radcliffe Hospital

The Radcliffe infirmary site is currently being redeveloped, the hospital facility having now been transferred to Headington, a village on a hill above Oxford. There are hollows, tunnels and secret chambers and facilities under Headington hill as well as beneath much of the surrounding area. They've installed a stone circle at the new hospital in the roundabout at the entrance. The old Radcliffe site is guarded by Gurkhas.

---

[20] Radcliffe Observatory: http://en.wikipedia.org/wiki/Radcliffe_Observatory
    I discovered the Maltese Cross top on Google Maps: Type in: OX2 6HJ to see the area.
    Cecil Green: http://en.wikipedia.org/wiki/Cecil_Howard_Green

Goodwill hunting?

On 17th November 2008, at midday, I was driving towards Headington on the A40 dual-carriageway, four miles east of Oxford. I had a passenger and we were in the inside lane when a big black Mercedes sped past us and then, just a few yards past us suddenly braked hard and sharp, for no apparent reason. As I looked across I noted the dark-tinted windows but what really caught my attention was that although I could see into the car, I could not see anyone driving; in fact I could not see anyone in the car at all.

About half a mile on we had to turn right so I drove into that lane and pulled up at the traffic lights; the other lanes began to flow through towards the Headington roundabout and as they did so I waited for the Mercedes to come along again. As it passed by the light from the other side of the car briefly confirmed that there was indeed nobody at the wheel.

There was something decidedly sinister about this incident; it was as if the car was seeking someone or something. Mercedes means grace, goodwill. There was nothing that felt 'good' about it.

Three
CONFERENCE

Probe International

Jean and Sam Wright

The multidimensional PROBE International conferences are run by husband and wife team, Sam and Jean Wright, a wonderfully warm couple who quickly make everyone feel at home. Their eagerly awaited, twice-yearly conferences are attended by hundreds of people from all over the world and are always informative as well as friendly. The 'PROBE International conferences are held in St. Anne's, Lancashire' and they are one of the largest seminars of its genre in the UK.

Many excellent speakers have presented their information to audiences at Probe over the years. It is a terrific resource for anyone who is looking for a more expansive view of this world or, for whatever reasons, is dissatisfied by the mandatory, authorised version of realty. Speakers on every topic and from all walks of life - academia, government, medicine, military, science, mysticism, entertainment, they all speak at Probe, whistleblowers too.

They are not the Gene and Sam from the TV programme 'Life on Mars' in case you're wondering - but knowing their lovely sense of fun - they'd love the action.

Death lie silence

Sadly, the October 2006 PROBE International seminar will go down in the annals of the global truth movement - and conference lore - as the day a speaker dropped dead in front of his audience.

Dean Warwick had been a late addition to the speaker line-up. A genius New Zealander who had excelled at engineering and sports he had worked for several governments in covert ops and after 30 years of silence had decided to come out and tell what he knew. He was a brave man. Only two weeks previously he had given an interview to journalist Dave Starbuck.[21]

This is how PROBE announced Dean's presentation in their pre-conference promotional material:

Dean Warwick:

An Inventor/Designer, Engineer/Researcher and Fighter for Freedom of Speech. He holds so many awards, they are too numerous to mention here. He is a most remarkable man. His talk will include his association with USA Intelligence, including the assassination of Robert Kennedy. (He was close at hand) and Dean is about to name the Anti-Christ.

Dean will open with a live Demonstration on himself - ILLUSION or REALITY?[22]

I spoke at Probe on the Saturday morning and I met Dean afterwards. He seemed lively and very chatty. He said that he had something that he must tell me but we were interrupted and I never did get to hear what it was.

I wasn't there but several people who were told me that later, in the speakers' room, Dean expressed his personal security concerns, saying, *'I must stay away from the windows. Any minute I am expecting a red dot on my forehead!* Some people thought 'Ay up! We've got another one of those paranoid blokes here' looked skywards and let it pass. Warwick also mentioned that his wife would have been with him but she had decided to stay at home instead after a premonition regarding a tragedy - thinking that it was something that would occur at their home in the borders of Scotland.

To add some authenticity to Dean Warwick's claims of working in secret ops he recognised a person with an ex-military background at the conference correctly stating where he'd seen him before. The other person was stunned having never mentioned that posting to anyone ever.

The presentation prior to Mr Warwick's was by two chaps from BUFORA (The British UFO Research Association), Stan & Richard Conway. Part of their show was a demonstration of a flying saucer using some fangled technology. I was told that one member of the audience

---

[21] A CD of which is available here: www.revelationaudiovisual.com
[22] www.ivy-rose.co.uk/Holistic_Events/498.htm

who asked what would happen if he were to put his hand under the UFO was informed his hand would disappear or disintegrate. Someone else has told me that this wasn't the case but that the man was warned that he would get a powerful shock as there was 20,000 volts round the thing! I can't tell you much more because I missed all but the last 5 minutes of their talk.

I unintentionally missed the first few minutes of Dean's talk and came in to hear him offering an animated, spell-binding (and convincing), argument against the official 911 story. *'The physics just don't add up'*, he insisted. *'How can a 110 storey building collapse in less than 10 seconds without some kind of additional assistance?'*

He told us that back in the 60s they were experimenting with demolishing buildings using sonar, and he suspected that this was the likely cause of the towers collapsing so tidily into their own footprint. He moved to his right and began introducing another topic, and then he stopped, flicked his hand in the air, turned and said, *'Oh before I do, I was going to tell you about Bobbie Kennedy. . .'* Without a warning he collapsed onto a table, resting on his left elbow and clutching his upper stomach he panted, 'Give me a moment . . . ' then toppled forward, hitting the floor with a loud bang. His head was cut but it did not bleed. Determined efforts were made to revive Dean as were frantic endeavours to call emergency services, but to no avail. I *saw* the life force go out of Dean as his body broke contact with the table. One person who rushed to Dean's side told me that there was a man in attendance who said that he was a professor (of something to do with medicine) who said that this was not like any other heart attack that he had ever seen. This was supported by a hospital porter who was there too, yet according to an autopsy Dean was judged to have died from a massive heart attack and a blood clot to the brain.

Was Dean taken out? He claimed that he had survived several attempts on his life and had received a number of them leading up to the conference.

According to Dean's driver, Mr Warwick had suffered a heart problem not long before. Perhaps this previous brush with mortality was what impelled Dean to blow the whistle on what he knew before it was too late. Dean dropped dead in the precise spot that the UFO demonstration had been performed just a little while earlier.

Also at the conference, and clearly shaken by the tragedy was the man who had encouraged Mr Warwick to speak to Dave Starbuck and the PROBE conference. His name is James Casbolt, whose family, he says, is steeped in the Secret Services. James says he is a renegade (and implanted) former MI6 operative intent on exposing the nefarious activities that he was once a part of. I am able to see auras and can confirm that James has very peculiar smoky-grey intrusions in the aura around his head. Most people now have implants somewhere. James has a website: www.jamescasbolt.com

James told me that Dean had intimate knowledge of underground bases and malign ET influence upon our governments and our world. He said that Dean was extremely troubled by recent global events, like the Twin Towers attacks and the subsequent wars in Iraq and Afghanistan because he had seen plans for these operations many years ago. That they had now occurred suggested to him that the rest of the agenda is about to unfold, to wit that there really is a death-planet heading our way and that as it closes in on us it will cause widespread mayhem and destruction. His information was that most of the population of Earth will be wiped out succumbing to colossal flooding as the Earth tips. This approaching planet, Niburu, is apparently already affecting other bodies in our solar system. Dean said that this is known by the controllers of this world and that it will happen before 2012.

James has also received confirmation from a contact in the shadowy world of covert operations that Dean was silenced using an E.L.F (Extremely Low Frequency) weapon.[23]

When we returned to our hotel that evening I noticed that the room door of the person who Dean had claimed to have met in Scotland was ajar. I know he'd shut it. Was it only a thoughtless cleaner . . . or was it a little message?

Just as in the case of Dr David Kelly's widow, Dean's wife says she is satisfied with the official version. Who can blame them?

David Kelly

Dr David Kelly's lack-blood body was discovered against a tree in a place that's name, 'Harrowdown' means High Altar. It was 17th July, about 11 days into 'the Dog Days' when ancient traditions say that Sirius (the

---

[23] www.thetruthseeker.co.uk/article.asp?id=5337

Dog Star) brings unbearable misery and evil. Dogs were sacrificed to the star, which is associated with the Egyptian God of the Dead, Osiris and his sister Isis - which some old maps call the River Thames here near Harrowdown. Kelly vanished on the feast day of Osiris' brother - the Dark God 'Set' and his body was discovered on their sister Isis' birthday. Kelly's middle name was 'Christopher'. St. Christopher was traditionally depicted as dog-headed, a cynocephalus, as was the Egyptian death inspector and embalmer, Anubis - *He who is upon his mountain* - (cf. Kelly's role as a biological warfare expert and weapons inspector and where he died), son of Set and his sister, Nephtys. [24]

A dog-headed
St. Christopher

The official story is that Kelly had slashed his wrists with a blunt knife (later police admitted that the knife had no finger-prints on it) and swallowed the Dark Moon number (29) of co proximal tablets - though nothing like this amount was found in his body. (See page 155)

Blue light

One early summer evening, in the late 90s, I was at a barbeque in a north east suburb of Perth. There were perhaps 30 or 40 people standing chatting in the garden when a huge, quick blue-white flash illuminated the dark skies; everybody stopped talking and looked towards where the flash had come from. Seconds later an even bigger blue-white flash exploded into the skies, the air fizzled audibly and so did everyone's skin. It lasted longer than the first flash and then visibly appeared to suck back into a spot far on the horizon, in the hills near Armadale, south east of Perth (directly south from us). Amongst the party were active and retired military personnel who said they'd never seen anything like it before. A few days later a retired Indian army officer, a neighbour of a relation, also reported the event - which was more than the media did; they never said a word! [25]

---

[24] Osiris, Isis, Nephtys and Set were siblings, children of the Earth god Geb and sky goddess Nut. Their feast days were considered and marked as, 'days out of time' in the Egyptian calendar.
St. Christopher as dog-headed: www.ellisctaylor.com/dgroystoncave.html

[25] In January 2009 reports of mysterious blue flashes are being made across north America - New York, California, New Jersey, Oregon, Indiana: www.examiner.com/x-2363-Chicago-UFO-Examiner~y2009m1d16-Ohio-man-reports-bright-flash-of-blue-light
Harry Mason: www.ellisctaylor.com/brightskies.html

Cornwall UFO Group Conference

Dave Gillham speaking at his conference and right, with a mate.

The following weekend after the October '06 Probe conference saw me at t'other end of the country, in Truro, Cornwall for the Cornwall UFO Group's 10th anniversary conference.[26] It was well worth the trip; a guaranteed weekend full of fun and fascination. Dave Gillham, the organiser and founder of CUFORG is a one off, self-effacing and the epitome of enthusiasm. His, and his intrepid *partner in crime*, Mike Freebury's lecture on animal mutilations in the south-west of England stole the show, it was stunning. Definitely not for the faint hearted, not just because of the horrific images of butchered animals - thankfully not many (I looked away) - but because of what they saw and photographed during their night time excursions onto the moors - 'orrible things hitching a ride in the back seat of Michael's car being just one of them.

Mike had returned home after one night on the moors and immediately experienced problems with his electrics. 'Not surprised,' replied Dave during a phone conversation, 'Have you looked at the photograph of your car? Look what's sitting in the back!' The photograph shows two beings that reminded me of the skeletal *victim* readers may have seen in the Bohemian Grove sacrificial rite video 'the Cremation of Care'.[27]

Jason Andrews was due to speak on the Sunday but owing to his wife's sudden illness and subsequent hospitalisation he had to call off. His mum, Ann, Phil from the Norfolk UFO Society and *yours truly* filled in.

The whole Andrews' family saga is one of, perhaps the, most intriguing, well-witnessed and documented cases of supernatural intrusion. Most everyone who has listened to Ann, and latterly Jason, speak would agree with that.

---

[26] www.cornwall-ufo.co.uk/2006
[27] www.infowars.com/bg_photo_gallery.html

The International UFO Congress, Laughlin, Nevada

I'd never been to America and after the paranoia that set in there after 911 it wasn't somewhere that I had any inclination to go to. I'd been told by people I know about the harassment and overt intimidation that passengers were subjected to and, to be honest, I couldn't be arsed with it. In order to safeguard freedom apparently they have to take it away.

The shame is that America is a land of breathtaking beauty but the promise of its people is made toxic by its greedy and corrupt culture in every shade from black to grey; a virulent culture that is relentlessly laying waste to nature, preying on humanity, destroying individuality and depleting the world's resources - there goes my U.S. book sales. But it isn't the people; I keep saying that because I know that it is true. Human Beings in their essence, without the macabre exertion that spews forth from the *Darkness*, are exalted creatures. If only more of us would realise that.

For years now friends have been urging me to go to the International UFO Congress in Laughlin, Nevada and I never wanted to go. I'm not really interested in train-spotting UFOs anyway but over the years UFO conferences have evolved to take in all matter of subjects that relate to other cover-ups so, against my better judgement (and because America is an 8-continent in an 8-year) I ended up going. This last minute decision set in motion a particularly sharp series of tests for me which mobilised the controllers, spoilers, pedants and *jobs-worths* (4-things) especially in airport customs, baggage-handling (launching actually) and security (also 4-things). [28]

I arrived a couple of days early after flying to Las Vegas via Los Angeles from London. We'd flown north from Heathrow, over the Isle of Lewis, across Greenland, down through Alaska, Canada and to California. The scenery for much of the way was incredible. The unusually cloudless skies over the north afforded long views of great white swathes of ice and snow, mountains - rocks on land and ice on sea before small settlements, oil wells and other intrusions heralded the opaque clouds that were to obscure much of the rest of the journey. An immense grid pattern of perfect squares (4s) drawn in the snow and ice became obvious before these blinds rolled over.

---

[28] Numerology: Please see Living in the matrix www.biggyboo.com/matrix.html and In These Signs Conquer www.biggyboo.com/signs.html

From Las Vegas I was the only passenger on the red-eye shuttle bus to Laughlin, me and the driver whose bearing and chatter swayed towards government interest. I didn't. I thought he looked a lot like the ex-CIA man and self-styled Alien-Hunter, Derryl Simms. Originally I was meant to make this part of the journey with my friends Mike Oram and his partner Fran but their plane had been delayed.

Soon after I arrived at the Aquarius Casino Resort, where the conference was to be held, I'd hopped into one of the six lifts en route to my (number four) room. Within seconds the lift was playing up - which from then on was a regular occurrence - for me anyway. (One attendee actually declined to get in the lift with me because, he said, the elevator seemed to go wrong whenever he'd been in one with me. Mind you he did know about my *otherworldly* experiences by then - I hadn't told him!)

I'd chosen a room for non-smokers, on a floor for non-smokers so I was surprised to smell strong cigarette smoke when I entered my room. I turned the light switch on and the bulb blew. I hung up my clothes and went into the bathroom turned round and saw a middle-aged woman walk past the door smoking a cigarette. I quickly dashed into the room but nobody was there. This spectral smoking-woman was in my room for most of my stay and I think she may have had company sometimes too. I was regularly awoken by conversations inside my room and it certainly wasn't coming from any adjoining room because the one good thing about this hotel was the first-class sound-proofing.

I hit the sack pretty quick not having slept for about 27 hours but little did I know that one of the rarest things I would encounter on this journey was proper sleep. Throughout my time there rolling waves of some sort of energy moved through my room accompanied by a low hum and this was exasperated by the stifling staleness that I could not describe as air being pumped through the room where none of the windows opened.

Every day my energy levels depleted a bit more. Early nights and early mornings became the norm. Several people told me that they were experiencing the same exhaustion. Many took to days, or a few hours, out: trips to the Grand Canyon, Oatman 'ghost town', Area 51 et al. Others, like me, took to their beds fruitlessly trying to catch some shut-eye.

Was it laser physicist and remote-viewing specialist, Russell Targ or psychologist Leo Sprinkle who mentioned during their talk how casinos deliberately install all manner of mind-control schemes within their establishments to keep people chained to their tables, wheels and machines? Some of which, they said, was intentionally designed to interrupt and disarray people's psychic senses. A ploy which, if true (and I think it is) clearly demonstrates how the *Darkness* fears this potent ability in humankind. Casinos, which are wholly owned by *Darkness*-motivated people, are undoubtedly a testing ground (and altar) in the ongoing assault on humans - and I don't care whether they are, on paper, owned by Native Americans or not. Physicist Russell Targ and psychologist Leo Sprinkle gave brilliant presentations. On the fourth day Targ conducted two (shortened) remote viewing exercises with the audience and some people achieved remarkable successes. In hind sight I wonder what the success rate would be had they conducted the experiments on the first and the last day? My efforts were pretty good though I was disappointed. I was hoping to replicate my success with the online psychic test on David Kingston's University of Life website where I got 100% but it wasn't to be. I got all the elements of the object we were asked to describe but didn't manage to put them together - Ann Andrews did well though.[29]

When Leo Sprinkle was giving his talk huge pink orbs and a *being* I have seen on several occasions, who I call 'the Councillor', accompanied him on stage. I don't know whether Leo realised this and although I talked with him a couple of times (a really lovely guy) I was so knackered I didn't think to mention it. We weren't permitted to take photos during presentations (I suspect because the DVDs they would be flogging would be affected) so I missed out on the chance of capturing lots of the phenomena that I could see.

Another incident happened when I was sitting with Mike Oram and Fran during Rob Simone's interview with Dan Burisch on the final day. As soon as Area 51 was mentioned I noticed a very tall, slight, white *being* stand behind Mike. It seemed to be fiddling with what looked like a black box or buckle at tummy level with its hands. The being may have realised that I could see it because just as swiftly as it appeared it disappeared. I felt it was male.

Something else that was strange happened when I was sitting near the front with a young couple from Arizona. Suddenly the floor began to vibrate and heave violently. (Only days before there had been a strong

---

[29] Leo Sprinkle: http://en.wikipedia.org/wiki/R._Leo_Sprinkle
    Russell Targ: http://en.wikipedia.org/wiki/Russell_Targ
    David Kingston's University of Life: http://universityoflife.users2.50megs.com/page25.htm

earthquake not too many miles from here.) The young lady was clearly very frightened, her partner and I weren't too chuffed with it either but nobody else in the room seemed to notice. It happened three times during the lecture and we nearly made a run for it. Afterwards we asked other audience members if they had felt it. Nobody had. The next day I was again sitting near the front but about 2 or 3 rows back from the day before when the floor began to *break-dance* again. The two people next to me could feel it but yet again nobody else seemed to. When I looked around the couple from the previous day were about 3 rows back from me. I gestured to them but on this occasion they could feel nothing.

On the Wednesday morning Ann, Paul, Fran, Mike and I drove into the Lake Mead Recreational Area National Park to a place called Grapevine Canyon, just a few miles from Laughlin, to see some Native American petroglyphs. There are hundreds of them there, mainly geometric but quite sparsely interspersed with more natural, seemingly foreign figures. Some of the glyphs may be thousands of years old. Clearly this was a shamanic site of huge significance. I hoped that this might be a profound journey for me yet I felt such little connection. It was beautiful and it was awesome yet no messages came to me. Just one small insight: that this was a journeying place where shamans from far and wide were welcome. They came in body or in spirit and they left their marks - the glyphs that decorate the granite slopes and crevices. Grapevine Canyon lies at the base of Spirit Mountain - don't you love that name?

Something very special happened to me on the Thursday. A lovely lady of mixed and mysterious Native American lineage gave me a beautiful carved brooch inlaid with crystal that she had made herself. She confirmed that the Grapevine Canyon site was indeed a shamanic journeying place.

During my trip to America, and to Sydney and Perth, Australia afterwards, I recorded my observations and feelings in my blog. As I have now deleted the blog (due to access hassles) I am including them now in this book:

Friday, 22 February 2008
Report from Saturn's Underpants

I'm on the road again and on the last day of Aquarius I landed at an hotel of the same name to attend the International UFO Conference in Nevada. Not quite the Age of Aquarius but this satellite of Las Vegas is definitely a leading attraction for the aged of Aquarius. Decadent and the epitome of naff, I find it strange that one of the foremost truth-seeking conferences in the world, one which encourages the higher ideals of humanity, takes place in this sink-hole of human potential and environmental resources.

Occupying the same crack in time and space (ahem) the US spiked a rogue satellite, the moon eclipsed large and earthquakes were set off around the world.

I had watched four films on the flight; two of them featured (probably unpaid) actors who brought another dimension to the storylines - orbs. A terrific orb posed during John Dee's appearance in 'Elizabeth' while we were treated to a more animated performance in 'The Assassination of Jesse James by the Coward Robert Ford'. While Jesse James stood next to his bed a bright orb drifted out from beneath it and determinedly headed upwards in an elegant arc. The film makers must have seen these orbs. Why did they leave them in? [30]

I wanted to see snow this winter. We flew over the Isle of Lewis, Greenland and Alaska and because there was less cloud than normal I got my wish. The scenery was stunning...and also puzzling - in Alaska. Why was the land marked out, in every direction and for mile upon mile, in grid squares like on a map?

It took around 27 hours for me to get from the frosty-white gown that Bridget had cloaked upon her Beloved Isles to the neon wastelands in *the Underpants of Saturn* (Underpants of SAturn). It would have been 8am if I'd lingered in *Blighty* and I needed to sleep.

My first sight on awaking in my hotel room was waves upon waves streaming diagonally across the room towards me - all entirely visible. Even when I closed my eyes and opened them they persisted. They weren't in the bathroom but when I returned to the main room there they were, rolling waves of energy that reminded me of a birds-eye view

---

[30] According to someone who watched the DVD version the orb isn't in that. So make of that what you will. However, if any reader does have a copy of the film with it in I'd love to hear from you.

of an ocean (without the white horses). That afternoon I was walking along 'the strip' with friends when I spotted the Aquarius Resort's sign - there in plastic and neon were the interminable waves that invaded my room. Seems the decadent excess of a serpentine sign really was/is enlightening us to what is happening within its lair!

Sunday, 24 February 2008
Sages of Aquarius

Well, that's the first day of the conference over. So far it has lived down to my expectations which, and I am sad to say it, were well below the enthusiastic reports I'd heard from friends for the previous 10 or 11 years - so maybe it's me... but anyway:

Yesterday most presentations were about ufological and philosophical fossils. The 'Aged of Aquarius' epithet from my last post is applying just as easily to most of the criers and denizens of this conference at *the Laughing Snake* (Laughlin = Laugh - lin = snake) who are about as avant-garde as a seized up wheel. Come to think of it, no wonder there are so many snake-oil merchants here. It's an eye-opener. It isn't substance and truth that impresses here it is brashness, loudness and what seat one has scrambled to on the reptilian ferris. Not that everyone here doesn't think they are disciples and dispensers of Love and Truth because they nearly all do before they barge their way into the lifts, puff their chests and credentials, or switch into car salesman mode attempting to flog you the latest fashion in Emperor's apparel. One speaker stated that good and evil people are present in every group. I was waiting for him to call out, "Hands up everyone who is evil!" But he didn't. That was a shame. I met a cyborg though.

This is a machismo world, where Saturn rules supreme - and surreptitious. Supercilious, superficial - and soporific to those who are of the Goddess - and there are a few of us here. On the first day (Saturday), the Goddess' first salvo shone through Nancy Talbot. Although her voice could strip 7 layers of paint in a blink her spirit, compassion and (I felt, under-appreciated) mystic qualities blazed through this darkened auditorium. Nancy's talk featured her research into consciousness, with amazing photographs of light phenomena and manifestations of thought on film. [31]

I know today is going to be better. It has been already. I think I have just watched a half-hour of one of the most important new films for humanity, a dramatised documentary of the Andrews family produced by real2cam films. [32]

Long time readers of my website will be aware that the Andrews' are friends of mine. They are friends not just because we share the same experiences but because they are lovely, kind and authentic people. Their story is rock-solid true, their message crucial. Jason - Ann and Paul's son - who is the main focus of their story, is interviewed at length in this docu/drama. I agree with everything Jason says in it as well as his obvious frustration with the limitations of *literation*. This spell-binding film oozes charm, wisdom and truth. It is inspirational beyond words and enlightening beyond conscious perception. If you get it you'll get it. Ann Andrews is going to be speaking at this conference later this week but for today we have another friend who I respect in equal measure, another messenger from the stars, Mike Oram.

Tuesday, 26 February 2008
Bulletins

Yesterday, while I was in the local supermarket, I heard the door open and a customer ask the shop assistant,

"Do you have any magazines?"
"No," the assistant replied...
"Oh, do you mean reading magazines?...No, we don't."

Gun culture!

6th March 2008
I've got one!

Well, the conference improved. I met some wonderful people too. The two guys from 'the Alagash Incident', Jim Weiner and Charlie Foltz, were just great. Their story, told with wit and aplomb, is both cautionary and fascinating. [33]

---

[31] Nancy Talbot's website is: www.bltresearch.com
[32] www.reality-entertainment.com/films/titles/walking-between-worlds-belonging-to-none
[33] The Alagash Incident: www.artgomperz.com/a1999/mar/alagash.htm

Singer Robbie Williams and the documentary maker, Jon Ronson attended the conference, and interviewed several speakers including Ann Andrews who didn't recognise Robbie till the end of the long interview. Double 16 (numerology), Robbie had a glowing energy entirely at odds with his media presented persona and although his career has been amazing this far I think  he is destined for far more significant things. It's up to him and we'll see.

The venue was appalling and the waves of negative energy that permeated the place that I reported upon earlier, continued. Countless people told me of, and I witnessed, their severe energetic depletion, lack of sleep and disharmony in relationships. I heard talk that the venue may be changed for next year - just why it has been held in such a hell-hole is as much a mystery as the subjects of the talks. (It hasn't been - same place again.)

Ross Hemsworth, who runs Glastonbury internet radio, was introduced as Europe's Art Bell or Jeff Rense - which raised a titter amongst the Brit' crowd and an, *'Oh, that's who he is'* from the rest. Ross gives a good presentation though some of his research was a bit dodgy I think. Nevertheless it gave food for thought, which is always a good thing. He showed a picture someone took of him in Rendlesham Forest (where the infamous UFO incident is claimed to have taken place). Above him, and to his left, Ross said he could feel 'a presence' and so asked a companion to take a picture. What came out was a remarkable *otherworldly* head with appendages to its sides. Ross thought it was *an alien* but the Woodbridge area is an extremely ancient shamanic site (Sutton Hoo etc) and I saw something else - Cernunnos (sometimes aka 'Herne the Hunter') [34]

It may be that Ross was given a huge clue as to the origin of the Rendlesham Incident that he hadn't recognised. A lady got up during questions to ask whether he'd considered Sutton Hoo - but Ross hadn't heard of it just as I suspect most other UFO researchers haven't. Ross was busy so I mentioned Cernunnos, and who he was, to his partner Penny.

---

[34] Cernunnos: http://en.wikipedia.org/wiki/Cernunnos

Maybe Ross will put this amazing picture up on his blog or perhaps it is in his book, I don't know. (Ross is now a director of the International UFO Congress and has a TV show out of MK Ultra (Milton Keynes) - on Edge Media TV; I watched it one night and a very good show it was too, the guests were Malcolm Robinson of Strange Phenomena Investigations (SPI) and former priest, current magician, Mark Townsend.[35])

I had an opportunity to make a break for it from Laughlin a day early so I took it and made for Las Vegas by way of Area 51 with Paul and Ann Andrews and two other friends James and Lynn. Area 51 was what you hear about it - ominous and oppressive. We saw some curious chemtrails and cloud activity including something that put me in mind of a sight that Paul Brandon and I had from Garsington Church - a plane following a dark line in the sky as it sprayed a chemtrail.

I had to wait till we got to Vegas before seeing a UFO. In a figure of 8 its lights alternated between the two loops. I grabbed my camera to snap it and the batteries fell out...jeees! It was dark and as I muttered something along the lines of, 'I bet by the time I've got these bloody batteries in it'll have gone'... it had.

Vegas was too much for a sensitive soul like me so I grabbed an early flight from there too and I write this from Sydney. I arrived yesterday morning - minus my luggage.

In Las Vegas airport I joined the snaking *blood-line* through customs where an official toady took my documents and exclaimed with glee, 'I'VE GOT ONE!' Another uniform bounds up and they both direct me to a glass-panelled room on the left.

"Why? What's the matter?"

"Just go to that room sir!"

[35] Sutton Hoo: www.suttonhoo.org
Rendlesham: http://en.wikipedia.org/wiki/Rendlesham_Forest_Incident
Edge Media TV: www.edgemediatv.com
Area 51: http://en.wikipedia.org/wiki/Area_51

I've already had my documents pored over and my stuff rolled through x-ray but here in the twilight zone it ain't enough it seems. So, off comes the shoes and the belt.

"Stand over there sir!" they say in their Gingerbread Man ferrying way.

"What's the problem?"

"Just stand over there sir!" came the delayed multi-echo.

Five minutes later there's a guy saying how he's going to pat me down and I'm thinking, 'wonder what would happen if I refuse?' And I'm tempted but because I realise that at the very least I will miss my flight I raise my arms dutifully. Two minutes later and I'm the right side of Vegas customs heading for home. Another hour or so to LA; 8 hours in the airport there, 2 hours sitting in a plane on the runway and 13 hours in the air sees me wandering bleary-eyed into Sydney Airport. I saw a whale though - just off Botany Bay.

And an hour or so later I'm reporting my no-show luggage to an airport lost-luggage bloke and he says he'll trace it. Well, the last time I saw my suitcase was a few minute before the used 'Jonnie' in Vegas called out, 'I'VE GOT ONE!'

Got what? Not a copy of the Universal Declaration of Human Rights that's for sure. It's an incredible document and I advise everyone to familiarise themselves with it.[36]

Well, it took another 6 weeks for my luggage to be located. Items of monetary value were missing, as were both padlocks although one had been replaced by a combination lock that anyone could have opened. Mind you something extra was in there a little 'Tough Shit' card from Homeland Security. That was nice.

---

[36] The Universal Declaration of Human Rights: http://un.org/Overview/rights.html

Here's something that occurred later in Perth, Western Australia:

4th April 2008
A thousand small wings beating

My first day in my old office in Western Australia... I had only been at the keyboard for about 30 minutes when suddenly I found myself reeling ... giddy, sick and with an excruciating headache. Almost blinded I stagger from the office and collapse on the floor...the walls and ceiling spin like white milk in stirred dark coffee and I close my eyes. I hear what sounds to me like a thousand small wings beating. I imagine a room full of butterflies. Slowly the nauseous feeling recedes, enough for me to cautiously open my eyes...I start to reach again, my head feels as if it is about to explode ...woom! Woom! WOOM! ... but I focus my imagination on the colours that I know I need and very gradually I recover - except for the headache that stays with me for the next 2 hours.

This had been a severe attack but not the first. I mentioned a similar incident (or was it more than one?) earlier. I'd felt its ire in Laughlin, a few weeks back, and another time sitting in this very same place back before I returned to *the Beloved Isles* several years ago. That time I had traced the cause to a malign beam of energy that had projected from a Telstra installation quite some miles away.

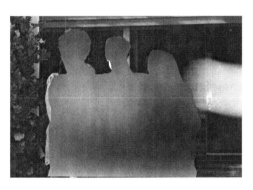

Energy beam penetrating my office wall.

I'd dowsed it; found out where it surged through the office wall and then later that same day, quite by chance, photographed it. Some work, involving such things as crystals, saw to it and I had no further trouble here ... till now. I'd forgotten about it, or at least put it to the back of my mind. This time though the beam knocked both me and the computer sideways - and that, dear correspondents, is why I haven't been able to respond to your emails. On top of this the ISP had a puzzling (their word) glitch in their system which caused their records of my patronage to disappear. Good hey!

* The people in the photograph prefer to remain anonymous. The picture was taken on a 35m film camera.

Marks of my ancestors

During my trip to Western Australia in April 2008 we drove down to the southwest and stopped off at the old church in Picton (Picton), near Bunbury, St. Marks, one that has so many historical connections to my family. As I wandered around the little church taking photos I felt the ghosts of my ancestors with me; orbs turned up in all of them.

And in Sydney in 2007:

27th July 2007
Sidh-n-ey perhaps?

At the beginning of June, still recovering from illness, I flew to Sydney. It was a long flight and the circumstances meant that not only did I get no sleep but I was also caring for four other people as well. I arrived completely exhausted - way past running on instinct and relying entirely on my psychic ability.

As I walked though Sydney airport I'd occasionally see figures rush past in a blur, too fast to be human. Now and again I'd catch someone staring at me; people who furtively glanced away or down at their shoes or quickly thrust a newspaper in front of their face - that sort of thing. There was one man who I kept seeing even out in the car park and later on at traffic lights well away from the airport.

Our group was met by friends of mine and I saw someone, a woman with a bizarre aura - it looked reptilian (green, scaly and throbbing). As I was running on the psychic part of me I, of course, did not dwell on these freaky events nor did I discuss them at the time.

The next day, still feeling *spaced*, I visited a Shopping Centre to buy a few essentials. The shopping centre is designed like something akin to a coiled spring: When rising you walk clockwise on the exterior and anti-clockwise on the interior.

Almost from the get-go nearly everyone I saw began to shiver and, curiously fluorescent they transfigured into strange beings with a green hue, wide and squat faces; some of them were completely naked. Most looked straight at me but every one of them kept walking. I noticed tails now and again. Every one retained their form at least until they passed me (I didn't look back). For the next 3 days or so, in diminishing regularity, I saw people shape-shifting in various parts of Sydney.

A few days later I was browsing through a magazine when I came across an advert for a film called 'Shrek the Third', which showed a picture of a baby *Shrek*. This, if it didn't have the long ears, would be a very close representation of the hundreds of beings I saw in that shopping centre in Sydney and at some other places there too.

Of course this shouldn't surprise me about Sydney really; it's the same city that was chosen to ring in the new millennium with its jaw dropping occult Olympic ceremony of pyramids, fire and sacrifice.

Nevertheless, if you like cities, there can't be many that can match, never mind better, this vibrant metropolis.

Reptilians

James Casbolt attended the Cornwall conference too and we chatted a few times. On one occasion he noticed the red patch on the base of my neck. He commented, *"That mark on your neck is a sign that you have been in the presence of reptilians."*

I've had the mark since 1996 when I had a string of *abduction* experiences that occurred almost every night for nearly two months. During this time I was left with various designs and finger marks on my body that my partner photographed and some of which I show in my talks. During this time a reptilian manifested in our dining room:

I was reading and listening to music in our lounge got up and walked across the corner of the kitchen. In mid-flow as I stepped through the door into the hallway I saw a giant bright, but olive-green reptilian creature crouching in the corner of the dining room - at least it would have been doing that if there was a corner; the room had disappeared.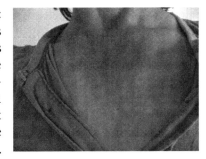

The creature was covered over most of its body with scales and it had yellowy-orange eyes. It looked as surprised to see me as I was to see it. I quickly turned back into the kitchen but it had gone and the room was back to normal.

James asked me if anything odd was happening at home and I mentioned the man who looked as if he had a shaven-head who I'd seen inside my house when I pulled into the drive but was nowhere to be seen when I got inside. "He was probably still in there," he said. They are aliens - hybrids, Zetans, and they have this box-thing on their belt that enables them to become invisible." Nice to know! And now it makes me wonder about the being I saw behind Mike Oram in Laughlin.

I've got a lot of time for James. I'm sure that not all of the information he passes on is true but I do think that he believes in what he is doing and that he believes what he shares could be vital for the inhabitants of this planet. He does what he can to verify what he can and that's as much as any of us can do. He isn't passing on fairy dust it is dangerous info, much of it and I think he's a courageous guy with a beaming heart. Much of what goes on in the shrouds of the vying factions that control our planet is impossible to verify anyway so what else can he do? Better to share what he's told than to keep it all quiet. James has written a fascinating book and he is offering it for free as an eBook. It is called 'Agent Buried Alive' and it's a bloody good read, see: www.jamescasbolt.com

Probe Conference October 2008

Sam and Jean Wright invited me to speak again at their wonderful Probe International conference in St. Anne's on 4th October 2008; and it was going to be even more special because my friend Mary Rodwell was going to be talking too. Yet even though I felt very blessed and honoured to speak at Probe, something that I couldn't put my finger on bothered me about it. As I've mentioned before I have had a very tough couple of years health wise - psychic and technological attacks being big parts of this and I was pretty certain that something would attempt to stop me from speaking there. I battled this feeling right up to the moment I said my first words on the stage there and then something happened. I could feel busy activity in the etheric spaces around me, I could sense something dark, determined and testing . . . and then I felt this calm . . . I felt wrapped in the strongest armour of Light and though I'd spent countless hours preparing a PowerPoint presentation I was almost at the end of my talk when I realised that I'd barely used it.

I'd also struggled with what I was going to talk about. Not that I haven't got plenty to say, it was more a case of how to knit it all together in as eloquent a way as I could.

I've always known that something of substance and viability must be built upon potent foundations and that includes some bloke getting up and banging on about how our lives are influenced, and directed, by beings that are not from round here. After all anyone can claim anything but, as several other experiencers have said to me, I have evidence; and it is all 24 carat. When one knows that LIFE IS VERY DIFFERENT TO THE ORDAINED REALITY, one has such an expanded view and vision that one inevitably questions everything that installed authority insists is true. It doesn't mean that you know everything but it can help you see what is hiding behind the bushes. Depending upon one's experiences they can also demonstrate the absolute certainty of the eternity of life and the illusion of death. This can make a person very dangerous to those with a vested interest in ensuring human beings are kept not only in ignorance but in servitude too.

There were a few dawns that saw me lying awake trying to come up with a talk for Probe that would achieve what I wanted it to do. Then on the Sunday evening, a week before I was to leave for St. Anne's, I attended the little Spiritualist Church in Oxford that I occasionally go to. Before the service, a woman who I know called me over and asked if I had any explanation for something that had occurred to her sister a couple of days earlier.

There are many ways that inspiration can be guided to you and as soon as this lady told me about what was puzzling her sister I knew with complete certainty that this was a message that had been sent to me. I'll explain, but first I want to tell you another true story:

An Angel in our midst

In 1997 I was living in Perth, Western Australia, most of my family were too but one of my brothers, his wife and 3 beautiful daughters - the youngest are twins - were still living in England.

It was December, winter time in England, and kids were sniffing and sneezing with the latest version of the season's ailments. Tyffany, just 9-years-old and the eldest, complained of a sore throat and feeling under the weather - a bit achy. She was taken to see the local doctor who gave her some antibiotics and urged a snug rest at home for a few days. As was expected she got a bit worse during the day. Her mum, dad and little sisters made sure that she was well looked after with whatever she needed, and made her as comfortable as possible. Later in the evening Tyffany went off to bed aiming to feel better in the morning. She loved going to school and playing with her many friends - she had missed them and wondered how they were getting on with the busy Christmas events and other things they were involved in.

In the middle of the night - the early hours, Tyff got up to go to the bathroom. Mum and dad heard her and got up to see how she was. She felt no better and in fact said she felt a bit worse; and just as we all say in such circumstances Tyff's mum and dad advised her to go back to bed and promised she'd feel much better in the morning.

Dad was up first - he had to be at work early. He popped his head round the door to see how his darling Tyff was. The shock and realisation was instant! He screamed and his wife darted out of bed. Tyffany had died in the night.

The devastating impact of losing a beloved child is indescribable. Nothing compares. Most of the family were in Australia but everyone knew Tyffany very well. She was one of those kids who shone -really shone. There was something very special about Tyff; and those were the precise words I left my brother with when I last saw her at their house in the November before she died.

As news of Tyffany's sudden passing reached her school friends and teachers tributes flooded into her family home. Little drawings, toys, poems and scores of letters relating how Tyffany had done something very special for them and how everyone loved her for the unique qualities she shared. Tyffany was a gifted artist and sportswoman. She loved football and could match and beat the boys on any day. She supported Newcastle United. Always she was there to encourage and support other youngsters who were experiencing tough times. Her smile had such serenity, and her aura . . . well it was tangible even to the most insensitive of people who encountered her. Just being with her I'm sure healed so many. We had an angel in our midst.

The family welded together. Absolute support and love poured from all of our hearts and into the little family unit back in England. Fortunately there were still some close family in England for my brother, sister-in-law and two nieces. One sister flew from America and another two siblings from Australia. The rest of us kept in constant contact by telephone. We were all heartbroken.

And it wasn't just the family, the whole village, the school and several amazing friends gained throughout my brother-and sister-in-law's lifetime united as one in support and grieving for the little girl who had given so much and the family she'd chosen to live with. Tyffany's head teacher describing Tyffany said, "She is an absolutely wonderful child with a little magic about her". The local newspaper, the 'Oxford Mail' showed a compassion and intelligence that is rarely seen these days in media. They were brilliant. I thank you all for everything you did.

Tyffany's funeral was held in the large village church. It was packed. The service included Tyffany's favourite song, "Together Again" by Janet Jackson, and a heart rending poem written and read by her cousin. Tyffany's grave brimming with flowers and piled high and wide with little treasures, favourite toys and keepsakes left by her young friends is still a frequent quiet place for many who still hold her memory in their hearts.

Those of us who couldn't make it to England for the funeral held our own quiet moments at the same time. We sent our love and our prayers to her mum and dad, her sisters, and to each and every one of us so painfully overwhelmed and feeling so bereft.

Although I hadn't attended church for a long time some months previous to this I had the urge to attend a spiritualist church in Perth. I'd never been before. I walked into the little church and sat down a few rows from the front cold winds flowed around my legs and I looked around to see whether there was a door open or air-conditioning on, there wasn't either. After a minute or so the winds vanished and I felt my hair moving. I looked around but there was no one close enough and then I heard breathless whispering in my ear. I couldn't understand what was being said. I enjoyed the service and went another couple of times before lapsing into my previous no-shows.

On the Sunday after Tyffany died it felt so natural to go to this little church in Maylands. I arrived about 5 minutes before the service was scheduled to begin and was surprised to find that the room was full - that was except for one complete row of wooden chairs to the right hand side as I faced the altar. I walked along the row of chairs to the wall but did not sit on the end chair, instead choosing the one before.

As I sat down my hands began to tingle and my skin broke out in goose bumps. A movement next to me, on my right, drew my attention . . . there on the chair between me and the wall was Tyffany. She sat there happy and smiling sitting on her hands and swinging her legs to and fro under the chair seat. She was wearing a football kit, but not Newcastle United's, a pair of white shorts, a blue football shirt, white socks and football boots. Tyff listened to the minister, giggling and looking around now and again and joined in energetically with the singing. At one point, in a quiet moment, she turned to me . . . I'll never forget it . . . she looked me in the eye and said, "Tell my dad I love him and I'm going to leave a white feather for him. He has to know that I will always be around." I felt a gentle touch on my arm, a sweet fragrance lingered for a heartbeat . . . and she was gone.

As I drove home I replayed everything in my head. I was elated, puzzled, excited and not a little apprehensive. Did I imagine it? If I didn't, why did Tyffany choose to visit me? She didn't know me as well as some other members of the family. But then, thinking about it, perhaps she knew me very well. This wasn't the first time souls who have passed on have come to me. Her message of love to her dad was entirely in keeping with her manner whilst she was alive. She knew, as I did, that her dad would be the one who found his grief the hardest to deal with. He has always been extremely deep, yet very emotional. She wanted to comfort him, instil some hope, and above all let him know that everything is all right. Did he blame himself? In such times it is easy to be irrational - to think that perhaps we could have done something that would have changed the outcome. Of course he couldn't have.

At first I didn't think about why she wanted to leave my brother a feather. I suppose I just accepted that it was . . . well, a present. But it is an enormously significant symbolic offering. It stands for peace and love, purity, harmony, acceptance, and for transmutation - perfect! And besides, Tyffany knew that my brother would surely need a physical sign to support the message she had charged me to deliver.

But, would there be a feather? It would, I pondered, have to appear in a circumstance that was entirely unusual. Otherwise who was to say that some bird hadn't dropped it or a pillow sprung a leak? I have to admit that the task of relaying a paranormal message to my distraught brother at such a sensitive time was not one I relished at all. Yet, although every part of me knew I had to, I wrestled with concerns about how this message would be received. Yes my brother is an open-minded person with unusual experiences of his own - but under these circumstances could he be expected to accept that his darling little girl appeared to his brother giving him a message on the other side of the world to pass on to him; and to compound matters the message could not be delivered in person. He would hear it by telephone. Would he feel that I was an insensitive brute playing hairy-fairy games at his expense?

In the end though I knew that my encounter with Tyffany was real; every second of it was etched into my consciousness. My fears and doubts had no place in what had to be done I had to trust that Tyffany knew what she was doing in every sense. So the next evening I phoned England . . .

My brother answered the phone, the tears and despair so evident in his voice. *"Hello Ell"* he answered. I silently prayed for the strength and eloquence to relate the circumstances and contents of Tyffany's message . . . and then began.

He listened to everything I said without comment. I don't know what I expected him to say really . . . there was silence, and I instantly suspected that I had made a huge mistake. We talked a little about what was happening and how they were coping. And then he said, *"I love you Ell - thanks."* A little light had pierced the sadness in that little corner of England - and Tyffany had been the one to do it again.

A few days later I spoke to my sister-in-law on the phone.

"Eddie told me about what happened," she said. *"He's been looking for a white feather wherever he goes."*

"Has he found one yet?" I asked.

"No, but he'll keep looking," she replied.

Jane sounded a little less fraught too. Perhaps the message had helped. I hoped it had. And I really wanted that feather to turn up.

A few days later I heard that my brother had arrived home from work, was about to step through the front door, when there right at his feet was a little white feather. He clutched the precious feather to his heart and his cheek, allowing a rare tear, gulped and rushed in to show it to his wife. The little white feather was tucked tenderly into his wallet - and there it stays to this very day.

But was this the promised gift from Tyffany? Maybe it was but then it could have got there by any number of means. I have to admit I did let an element of doubt creep into my mind. My brother felt it was that precious treasure - and who was I to voice doubts? It brightened his life and that meant more to me than anything my sceptical mind could propose. To my shame, though my lifelong experiences had continuously presented evidence that life is eternal, I had less confidence in the reliability of something I was intimately involved in than my brother had in the integrity of his older brother, and at a time when he far more than I was entitled to disbelieve.

Yet in my heart I did know, with absolute certainty, that I had had an encounter with an inspirational little girl spirit in a little church in Maylands, Perth, Western Australia; and that she had given me a message of love and hope which she had trusted me to pass on to her grieving dad: one that helped him and her mum to cope with the most terrible loss of all. I determined that I would accept that the little white feather was the one that Tyffany had declared to me she would leave for her adored dad. And that was that.

A few weeks went by, maybe a couple of months. Early one morning I grabbed my work clobber and hurried down the steps to my car. As I put the key in the car door I noticed right in the middle of the driver's seat . . . a large, pristine fluffy white feather!

I opened the door and carefully picked the feather up. How could it have got there?

Had little Tyffany left a feather for me too? She must have. She hadn't told me that she would but Eddie had found his. But was the feather my brother found the one that she had promised him. I was delighted, in awe, and confused about what I should do. I ran inside and showed it to my partner.

"It must be for you," she said. *"It's a thank you."*

I carefully carried the feather into my study, placed it on a shelf next to a photograph of Tyffany and said a quiet thank you. Sometimes I would take it down when I thought about Tyffany, her mum and her dad and sisters. And every so often I still wondered, "Is this feather meant for me?"

When I moved house I carried the precious feather separately to keep it safe. In the new house I kept it on a shelf in my study too. Then one day, for no apparent reason, I couldn't find it any more. I searched everywhere I could think of. Every room, cupboard, drawer, desk and even places I knew it couldn't possibly be, all over the house. I even searched the loft and the sheds; but the feather had disappeared. I asked everyone and racked my mind trying to locate it. I have always been so good at finding things but I couldn't find this. Only one place remained, my no-longer used travel bag that I used to use when I did readings at Psychic Fairs, and even though a picture of it kept flashing in my mind I didn't want to look there; because if it wasn't there then the priceless feather was gone. I avoided looking for weeks. Every day I would think to myself, "I'll have a look, it must be there." And I chastised myself frequently for being so careless. How could I lose something so wonderful, so miraculous? Who knows what effort was required to materialise a pristine white feather inside a locked car, on the driver's seat where it was sure to be noticed? I really couldn't face up to the loss. So long as I didn't look then I could always hold on to the hope that it was there, in the travel bag. Though I wouldn't have put it there I had to have hope.

Then one night Tyffany came to me in a dream. She thanked me for passing her message on to her dad and then said, *"There is going to be a new baby boy in the family."* That is all I can remember.

When I woke up I remembered the dream. Did she mean that Eddie and Jane were going to have a baby boy? They had been blessed with a little son since. No one, as far as I knew, was expecting a baby. I asked around the family whether anyone was expecting. No one was.

Several weeks later I had a phone call one day from England. The caller had spoken to my niece that day (the neice who had written and read the poem at Tyffany's funeral) - she had become estranged from her parents,*"I just had to call you. . ..I just realised. . .I was asleep. . .Nina told me today that she had just had a scan. She is going to have a little boy."*

"I didn't know she was pregnant." I answered.

"No one did," she replied. *"Not even her mum. I just had to tell you. I'm really tired and got to be up early tomorrow so I'll get back to sleep now."*

We said our goodnights and I put the phone down. I was feeling a bit perplexed.

"Who was it?" my partner called out.

"Oh, it was Louise, for some reason she woke up and had to tell me that Nina was going to have a little.." Suddenly it dawned on me. "That's it!" Louise had phoned to tell me that Nina was having a little boy because that was what Tyffany had told us would happen. Again Tyff had come through to present proof that she was still around - Yet more amazing confirmation for Eddie and Jane. It was a wonderful moment.

Of course after my dream of Tyffany I continued to wrestle with my questions and concerns about the feather but I still couldn't bring myself to look in the bag. Now though there was an increasing urgency. Every day I became surer that the feather was meant for my brother and this increased my dread of looking in the travel bag. In just a few weeks I would be flying to England and would be seeing my brother. I had to have that feather.

One morning, sitting pensively in my study the thought came into my head, *"Go and look in the bag now"*. I had goose bumps and not a little apprehension as I opened the bedroom cupboard. I wheeled out the bag, and knelt beside it. This was it. I had to allay my fears and face the music. The bag was stuffed with all sorts of odds and ends we never used. As I pulled these out I thought there was no way I would have put Tyffany's feather in here. If it was it would be crushed and completely ruined. In a way I hoped it wasn't there. Perhaps I'd left it at someone's house. One of the most likely scenarios was that it had fluttered down from my study shelf and been vacuumed up by mistake. I continued to pull stuff out of the bag until the only thing left was a papier-mâché round red trinket box with an outline of the Earth in gold upon the lid. Well that was it. I'd lost Tyffany's feather. There was no where else to look. I knew it was pointless looking in the trinket box I didn't put it there. I opened the lid quickly - dismissively really, when I noticed tucked nice and safely inside this eminently safe place was Tyffany's fluffy white, pristine feather.

I've since passed the feather on to my brother. He'll keep it safe. And every now and then he'll pick it up, like I did, and he'll know - as I do.

We have an angel in our midst.

***

The lady who spoke to me about her sister, in the Spiritualist Church in Oxford, is a relation by marriage. She told me that her sister was hanging the washing out a couple of days before when the words, "White

Feather" came into her mind; she looked on the ground and there was a beautiful little white feather.

Tyff wanted me to talk about her white feather . . . and that is what I rounded off my talk with.

***

I travelled to St. Anne's the next Friday night with a friend. On the way, at the last moment, we decided to use the M6 Toll Road. As we entered this motorway we both said that we'd stop at the service area to use the lavatory and get a drink . . . The next thing we were on the ordinary M6 motorway with a large van in front of us with a number plate that included the letter combination CIA. We both said, at the same time, "That's the same van that was in the petrol station back at Oxford!" Only then did we realise that we had missed the toll road's service station although we were sure we had both been keeping an eye out for it. We thought that maybe it wasn't there anymore - but it was undoubtedly there on the return journey. It seems that something unusual happened to us on the lightly travelled M6 Toll Road.

For the first time the Probe conference was held in a ground floor hall; previously the event was held in the same building, but upstairs. Unfortunately the acoustics and the sound-system struggled for the first 3 speakers and I was on second but it was sorted out and as a bonus, what the audience got instead were amazing *spectral spectacles* - the manifested *otherworld* activity that I could feel going on all around me. Numerous attendees came up and told me what they could see and some had taken photographs. I'm hoping they'll send them to me and permit me to either post them on my website or print them in a later edition of this book. My friend was shown some extraordinary snaps of luminosities circling my head and several people, independently described seeing the same entities around me. My friend, and an ex-serviceman attendee, independently described how when I showed one of my drawings a face came out of the screen and looked around the audience before receding back into the screen. I was told by a number of people that soon after I began speaking my aura was enormous.

Overleaf are two photographs of me talking at the Probe conference on 4th October 2008 - taken by a member of the audience.

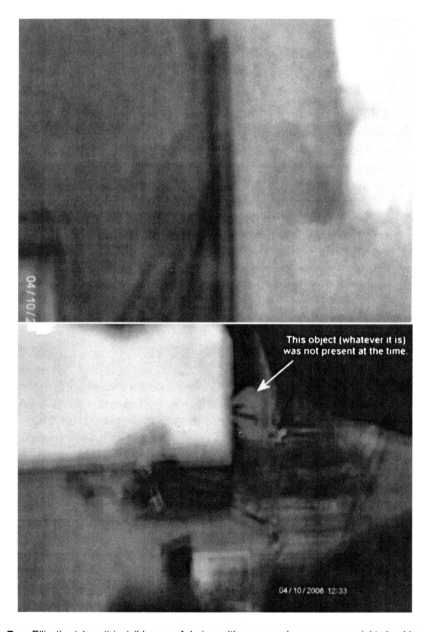

Top: Ellis, the (almost) invisible man. A *being*, with rays, can be seen on my right shoulder.
Below: There's so much going on in this photo. The 'white screen', which was behind me, has expanded and now intrudes into the front. Other *beings* share the stage with me, and there are also unknown objects beneath the 'screen' and across my chest.

I was there - honestly!

Whenever I speak at conferences something out of the ordinary seems to happen. A few times members of the audience have collapsed and I have been shown quite a few photographs of luminosities around me. A lovely young woman, Michelle Brereton, a 'paranormal investigator', sent me these photos that she took of me on her phone camera during one of the talks I organised in Oxford. I'm sitting down on the left. The lady said she saw some strange activity occurring around and above me, including a luminous being and a blue streak, so she grabbed her phone camera as quick as she could.

© M. Brereton

Visions

Like many people I sometimes receive visions that are to do with serious crimes. I have already mentioned some of them but here are some more:

Claremont

From a few days after Sarah Spiers vanished from the well-heeled Perth suburb of Claremont I had several visions and psychic clues concerning serious crimes.

Sarah, I was *told*, would not be found for a very long time. I had discussions with senior police officers regarding my psychic visions and information. One very senior officer took great pains to ensure that when we spoke we used a secure line. Why was that do you think?

I'm quite sure I 'saw' the circumstances of Sarah's abduction (see page 105) and started receiving psychic information mainly in symbolic language (e.g. lions, a pipe) that lead me to an area north of Perth where there used to be a lion park and close by a road called, Pipidinny Road. There were several very strange, chilling and disturbing incidents connected to this investigation and police were kept fully appraised of every psychic detail (and confirmation) that I received.

Five months later another young woman, Jane Rimmer, vanished from Claremont in similar circumstances. Again I received psychic information (e.g. rocks and a well). Jane's body was found - in a place called WELLard near ROCKingham.

In March, the following year, Ciara Glennon disappeared from Claremont. Her body was found in PIPIDINNY ROAD. The police officer in charge of the investigation at the time, speaking on television news, acknowledged 'one young psychic who had got very close'.

To date no one has been charged with these crimes.

A day and a half late

A young trail-bike rider had disappeared while out riding in bushland south of Perth. I sat down and meditated on it and 'saw' a young lad dressed in a leather jacket lying in undergrowth near to a stream. I could not see any helmet or bike but I felt that it was the missing teenager. I took out a map book and psychically located the spot where the lad was.

A news bulletin suggested that searchers were heading away from where the lad was so I telephoned Crime-Stoppers and gave them the coordinates. The lady said that someone would phone back. Nobody did and a day and a half later the body of the boy was discovered in the spot I had sensed -and reported to police.

A man and a woman were convicted for the young lad's murder.

Sarah Payne

I meditated on the disappearance of 8-year-old Sarah Payne after hearing about it on the radio and passed the information on to police. Several details were subsequently verified but my information was that three abductors were involved - two men and a woman. A man called Roy Whiting was convicted of little Sarah's abduction and murder. [37]

On 5th July 2000, 5 days after Sarah vanished, a picture crammed with occult suggestions, that the Sun newspaper said had been painted by Sarah, was published on the page normally touted for pictures of bare-breasted women, page 3. I came across it in odd circumstances.

On that day I was on my way to visit friends in Norfolk and arrived in Norwich very early in the morning hoping to find a café open. I was a little early for that but the garage next door was open so I decided to buy a drink and something to read from there. The only newspaper on show was the Sun, which is not a paper that I would buy but under the circumstances. When I queried the shop assistant about it he told me that he didn't know why but it was the only newspaper that had arrived that day. Back in the car, when I flicked through the pages, I could not believe what I was seeing; I felt a chill, one that has never left me to this day when I think about it. As soon as I could I made sure that the presence of this painting was known around the world. [38]

---

[37] www.ellisctaylor.com/psychicvisionssp.html

[38] Sarah's Painting: www.ellisctaylor.com/sarahspainting.html
and IN THESE SIGNS CONQUER p 210

Remote control

One morning, as I sat in my friend's lounge - where I was house-sitting - I kept thinking I must find the time to meditate. It was a couple of days after 11th September 2001. I felt something brush the back of my hair and I closed my eyes. A brilliant turquoise light, about the size of a pea, pulsed in front of my eyelids and grew steadily larger. A sense of loving calm washed over and through me. Then came the eyes: intense, white and wise. When I am about to receive a vision I always get the eyes:

I was inside an aircraft and although it was daylight all of the passengers were asleep, every one. Nobody was moving. I could hear the low hum of the aircraft. I noticed some Arab faces; one of them was late 30's/early 40's sharp, with a large pointed nose; another was more round faced, about early 20's, both were clean shaven and dark skinned and both were unconscious . . . and then it went. That is all I saw.

I immediately emailed a few close contacts including Lauren Savage, the then webmaster of www.davidicke.com to alert them that there was another possibility other than the rampant suicide-bombers media stories. In those days davidicke.com almost always carried my new articles. [39]

Of course this could be any airliner, almost anywhere but I was prodded to look and I felt this vision was telling me something important. I thought about it:

In all of the many times that I have travelled by air I have never seen all of the passengers asleep in a light-drenched cabin and I have never experienced everybody on a plane asleep at the same time. I have never been in an aeroplane where there is complete silence except for the drone of the engines. Always there is fidgeting.

The vision haunted me and I could only think of one reason that this situation could exist. All of the passengers must have been dead; an aeroplane flying through the skies with a lifeless human cargo. It's macabre. Were the pilots also dead? I don't know but it suggests serious possibilities about what happened on that fateful Tuesday on 11th September 2001.

---

[39] Lauren Savage runs the book publisher and internet bookshop, Hidden Mysteries who publish my First two books in America: www.hiddenmysteries.com

Suppose the Arabs were on a terrorist mission (or even an entirely innocent journey for that matter) and some shadowy group wanted to cause the mayhem that we are now witnessing. Suppose that the *'Shadows'* knew, for whatever reason that these people would be on the plane (they may even have bought their tickets for them, for all I know) - and we have *the patsies*. Then suppose they had pre-recorded a few messages (easy to imitate other peoples voices) to transmit (purportedly) to loved ones. Once the passengers were airborne either the air is switched off or more likely they are gassed (the passengers faces looked normal); the same thing happens to the flight crew and the plane is taken over by remote control. Impossible?

Well it wasn't long before military and industry professionals independently were suggesting that just this scenario was likely to be what really went on. [40]

---

[40] Vision recorded on www.ellisctaylor.com/Amattroc.html

Four
CONTACT

I was living in Perth, Western Australia and one day, for no particular reason, I decided that I would report a UFO that a friend and I had seen in the skies over the village of Fairford in the UK, in about 1988. I didn't know who I was going to report it to at the time so I looked in the phone book and lo, there was a UFO society in Perth. Then I forgot about it. This would have been around the time when I discovered the shaved area on my leg when I was having a shower one morning. I don't remember the date, but it was in March 1996.

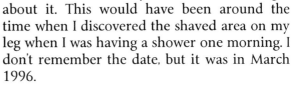

Other things were occurring then too: I noticed a red circle on my little step-daughter's leg and when I told my partner about it she told me that she had seen the same thing on me that morning. I woke up on some mornings after this with a red burnt patch around my mouth and nose in the shape of an oxygen mask.

On many nights I heard my name being called but when I opened my eyes nobody was there, when I decided not to open my eyes then the voices would say they would return later. I seemed to be affecting electrical things around the house. One day every one of my power tools burnt out. Watches stopped working on me. The television and stereo behaved oddly - I put a 45 vinyl record on the turntable - 'Solid Gold', a song written and performed by a friend of mine - and the player dispensed with his vocals playing only the music. Apparently this is impossible but I wasn't the only one to witness all these bizarre incidents happening around me.[41]

All my life I have experienced supposedly strange things and very often other people have been around to witness them with me.

In 1955, when I first came to live in England we lived in my Nan's and Gramp's big Victorian house, almost in the centre of town. I remember lots of things that occurred there - including some strange ones. I was no

---

[41] http://uk.youtube.com/watch?v=LMVSuJxxrGY

more than 4-years-old, but I can clearly recall watching a man dressed in a pilot's leather uniform walking down the stairs and through the wall on one of the landings. My sister saw him once too.

Another thing I can remember is lying in bed watching the door open slowly. As I sleepily peeked out from under the blankets a very strange looking face would peer around the door and shake its head up and down and then the door would shut. The visitor had quite a large head, a big hooked nose, a reddish face and a peculiar hat with a bell on it.

When the summer came we all went for a daytrip to the seaside. If we were very good, we were told, we would be allowed to watch the *Punch and Judy* Show. We didn't really understand what it was but it seemed so exciting.

My sister and I were busy making sandcastles when someone hollered, "Quick the show is about to begin!" And we all rushed to join the other kids in front of the striped tent. I can remember being dumbstruck when the curtains opened because there, up there, was my night time visitor. I don't remember much else about that.

Helicopter?

In 1961, when I was just 9-years-old, I was playing with some friends in the fields close to where we lived. It was during the summer holidays and it was a beautiful sunny day. We were very engrossed in our games but that doesn't explain how a helicopter could appear from nowhere and without making a sound but we were only kids and like most all kids then, technologically ignorant. How were we to know that helicopters are very noisy aircraft? We'd probably never seen one before, not that close anyway. It was only about 50 yards or so from us.

We'd met Americans before though and we recognised the accents of the occupants when they walked bolt upright out of the helicopter and asked us if we wanted to go for a ride.

That's all I remember. Happens to people all the time that . . . well, doesn't it? No? Oh!

We forgot about it immediately. We never mentioned it to anyone and we never spoke about it to each other. How strange is that! Can you imagine . . . the most exciting thing a kid could ever think of happens to them and they just forget about it? Gradually, as the years rolled by I began to remember but try as I might I could never recollect anything that happened between the pilots asking us whether we'd like a ride and us walking home.

What I recall is seeing the helicopter and two tall blond men in flying suits walking out - there was no stooping, no flaying hair just straight upright walking. For years as a youngster I felt puzzled when I watched people disembarking from helicopters crouching low and hanging on to their hats. 'They don't need to do that!' I used to think to myself.

The two pilots walked up to us, asked us if we'd like to go for a ride . . . and that's it, all I can remember. I knew they were Americans because just a little while before a softball team from the American base had visited the school and taught us how to play softball; and as we were all cowboy fans too when the pilots said, "Howdy" that clinched it.

I think it must have been a couple of years later that I started to remember some things. It happened when my best friend asked, *"Do you remember when me and you went on that helicopter and they took us for a ride over the car factory?"* I didn't, but he'd stirred something and the things I've mentioned already came back to me; but I still didn't recall anything about the car factory.

Near to Guy Fawkes Night (5th November - Samhain), at the other end of the field, with the same friends and others, we were out after dark building a huge bonfire when something huge and dark swooped over us and gave out a massive roar that seemed to reverberate all around. It terrified us and we all scarpered for home.

One summer night, it must have been about 11 years later, I went to Reading with my friend who'd remembered the helicopter ride. We hadn't seen each other for years but we'd bumped into each other the day before and we'd arranged to have a night out. The town of Reading is about 30-40 minutes from where we used to live, a new council housing estate near Oxford called Blackbird Leys. It was during the week and both of us had to be at work the next day. We met some Reading girls and ended up at their place after the pub shut at 10.30. Just after midnight we left for home taking the back road through the village of Nettlebed. We hadn't gone many miles when we drove into a patch of fog. I don't remember anything unusual happening but when we got home we were shocked to find that instead of it being about 1 o'clock it was nearly 4.30am!

Soon after this my friend and I both moved away and we lost contact but 10 years later I moved to a small village about 12 miles away and guess who was living there too . . . yep! Occasionally we would go for a drink together in one of the next villages and it was on one of these nights out that I asked him if he remembered the helicopter incident. He looked blank at first but then said, *"Yes, I do Ell, I'd forgotten all about that."*

"What happened mate?" I asked him. I didn't want to say what I could remember I really needed to know whether my recollections would match his, and they did. He too could recall nothing after the two men talked to us. "But can you remember flying over the car works?" I enquired. He couldn't and I told him how, when we were kids of about 11, he'd told me about how just he and I had been taken for a flight over the Cowley works. He still couldn't remember that so I don't know what went on there. I asked him if he could remember who was with us when we first saw the helicopter but like me that part was vague. There were lots of kids around in those days.

In the late 90s I visited the UK on holiday and met a mate in a pub that was being run by an old friend from my childhood. Both of them were ex-coppers funnily enough. I couldn't pass up the opportunity so just before I left I turned to my landlord friend and asked him if he was with us when we saw the helicopter? *"Yes, I remember that,"* he said, *"Those geezers got out and came up to us. I think they asked us if we wanted to go with them. . . "*

"Yes," I said, anticipating something more, anything. My friend looked at me with a puzzled expression . . .
"What happened next?" I urged.

"We probably ran away!" he said and hurried off without even a proper goodbye.

"WE PROBABLY RAN AWAY"? What the . . . ? 30 years ago something fantastic happened to a bunch of mischievous kids and at least 3 of them could recall only little bit about it but nothing more.

These strange incidents have always nagged at me and I mentioned them to my mate Mary Rodwell who suggested a regression. At that time I was a *somnambulist*, a cinch to put under, and a stream of detail concerning the helicopter incident came out. The regression is documented in Mary's book, *Awakening ~ How Extraterrestrial Contact can Transform your life!* [42]

Providing what came out in the regression is accurate the helicopter was not a helicopter at all and we didn't go for a jaunt over the car factory, at least that isn't the only place we went. My friend was right about one thing though, all those years ago, it was just me and him - unless others went separately of course.

I've tried regression a couple of times since attempting to retrieve memories of what occurred during the missing time events noted earlier in this book but a block has been installed and I have had no success yet.

Off his rocker

Summer 1969, about 2 o'clock in the morning, and my friend and I crept through the front door of his parent's house on Blackbird Leys. We'd been to a dance at Oxford Town Hall and walked the 3 or 4 miles back. Using only the light from a standard lamp in the sitting room Dave switched on the kettle to make a cup of tea. Leaving him to it I sat on the sofa next to the rocking chair picked up a comic and started reading it under the lamp. A little while later I heard Dave come in, sit down and begin gently rocking the chair next to me. I continued reading and came to a particularly funny part laughing out loud I handed the comic to Dave to look at . . . the chair continued to rock . . . but without Dave in it. Launching myself swiftly through the door to the kitchen there was Dave stirring the tea. "Did you just come in the sitting room?"

"No. Why?"

Ouija - Nonnein?

In 1973 I moved in with my girlfriend (to a number four house) I was 20-years-old. Not long afterwards, I can't recall why, but it was probably just for a lark, she, her brother, his friend and I decided to have a go at the spirit board. I don't think any of us had ever tried it before, I

---

[42] Mary Rodwell, *Awakening ~ How Extraterrestrial Contact can Transform your life!*, Avatar Publications (June 24, 2005)

certainly hadn't, and we didn't have a board; what we did have was a
pack of Lexicon cards. A spirit board (or Ouija Board) is a system used to
communicate with *otherworld* entities using letters, numbers and a
planchette (usually a wooden pointer) or upturned glass. Lots of people
are scared of using these devices and many experienced psychics and
metaphysicians do counsel against using them. We weren't aware of this
at the time though. [43]

Sitting around the dining room table we laid the Lexicon cards out in
alphabetical order in a circle and put an upturned drinking glass - a
whiskey glass I think it was - in the middle of them. We all put our right
fingers on top of the glass and I called out, 'Is there anybody there?' The
glass began to move immediately, I looked at everybody's faces where
there had been smiles there was alarm and I tried to lighten the mood by
making a joke zzztt! an intense heat shot from the glass and through my
finger . . . Yow! I yelled instinctively pulling my finger from the glass.
My companions faces drained to white but not one of them took their
fingers away - which is strange when I think about it now . . . and I,
suitably admonished, replaced mine. The glass began to move again and
spelled out 'YES'.

We 'played' with the Ouija a several times over the next few days
communicating with several entities. We asked one whether it could tell
the future and it said it could correctly predicting a bomb find in central
London the next week - the place and the day. We played card games
with it and it always won and it could always predict the top card in a
freshly shuffled pack, no matter who did the shuffling. The spirits told us
lots of things that, when we could verify them, proved to be correct. They
told us too that sometimes, when they want to manifest in our world
they become birds or trees.

We treated it all as a bit of fun but then one day a new visitor came
in. Something felt different about this one. I didn't like it and I noticed
that I felt sick and there was a heavy feeling over my brow; but I carried
on. This new communicant told us that someone I knew, but no one else
at the table did, had been murdered by her boyfriend in Ibitha and her
body had been hidden. I hadn't seen her for years and I didn't know
where Ibiza was - never heard of it, nor had the others. This sudden
change in the mood of the communications frightened us and we closed
the board. We found out over the next couple of days that Ibiza was the

---

[43] Ouija: http://en.wikipedia.org/wiki/Ouija
     Lexicon: http://museums.leics.gov.uk/collections-on-line/GetObjectAction.do?objectKey=264348

same place as Ibitha, a holiday island near Spain that we'd vaguely heard of as it was becoming popular to visit at the time; but we didn't recognise the spelling. I made enquiries after the person that the Ouija entity had told us had been murdered and thankfully they were perfectly OK.

I was really confused by all this. As far as I was concerned up till then our times with the entities (dead people we assumed and were told) had been just a bit of fun and they'd proved to be real, very real. On another occasion I'd again been irreverent and the glass (with our fingers on top of it) had leapt about two feet up in the air and crashed down on the table top - nobody was pushing this thing! and as far as I knew no one amongst us had x-ray eyes or a Tardis to travel into the future.

I'd had lots of supernatural experiences before I'd experimented with the Ouija but never before anything, as far as I can, or could recall, as disturbing as this had felt. We lived in a village near Oxford in the UK where we knew the local vicar who was a really lovely man and I decided to go to see him. We talked for a while and he told me that he knew of a number of people that were now in Littlemore Hospital after their terrifying experiences with demons that used the psychic energy concentrated through using the Ouija Board. He had made a personal study of these things and had discovered that usually one of the people in a spirit circle had a heightened susceptibility (these are his words) to psychic communication and that this can include demonic interference. He asked me whether I had had anything supernatural happen to me before and I told him that I had. He suggested that we prayed together and strongly cautioned that I never use the Ouija again. I felt better after this.

Around this time I was walking towards the bus stop when I saw an elderly man waiting there with another 2 or 3 people. I was about 20, or so, yards away when to my shock the man collapsed. I rushed over to him his skin was blue and he didn't seem to be breathing. I called out for someone to phone an ambulance and without knowing why I was doing it I put my hand on his brow and his chest. The man began to murmur softly and his skin seemed less blue. The next thing I knew the ambulance had arrived and the man was whisked off to hospital.

A year and a day

In 1975 I moved back to Blackbird Leys and every other Friday night I'd meet my mates at the Blackbird pub and we'd walk the 15 minutes together along the country lane to the Minchery Farm discothèque near

Littlemore. The last part of our route took us along what was once a Roman road and the building itself occupied part of an old Knights Templar priory site.

In its day the priory stood alone out in the lonely moors known as Little Moor (Littlemore). When we were children the buildings were ruins and home to scores of feral cats.

One bitterly cold still night I arrived at the Blackbird an hour late and was told that my friends had left 20 minutes earlier; declining a drink I hurried off after them. Leaving the bright streetlights of Knights Road I plunged into the inky haunted harrow. Even in daylight, at this time of year, the landscape looked like the wastelands of Arthurian legends. Not another soul was in sight and very soon the only lights

All that remains of the Templar priory at Littlemore. It was dedicated to St. Mary

were behind me. I had no moon to guide me but I'd travelled this way countless times before and I knew the way.

Clasping my coat collar around my neck and ears I passed over the small bridge where we kids used to fish for sticklebacks and walked briskly towards the corner where I would turn right. Just another 400 yards and I'd be in the warm. It was then that I spotted a white figure about 75 yards away walking across the field approximately at a right

It's a horse...no, it's a bloke in a white coat!

angle to me. I stopped both alarmed and puzzled by what I could see. The figure was moving through what I knew to be a field sparsely covered in weeds and long grass.

'It must be a horse', I thought, but if it was it was a human-shaped horse.

'Well, it's a bloke in a white coat then!'

No, it couldn't be. Every part of it was white and glowing. What's more the figure wasn't walking; it was gliding. Then it stopped! It turned . . . and I could see that it was now facing me. Suddenly it rushed towards me. I took off like a bat out of hell. I ran and I ran, faster than Linford Christie could dream of; but it felt as if I was wading through a whirlwind and getting nowhere. At any moment I was expecting something horrible to grab me. Breathless I burst into the disco lobby . . . and there, just paying to get in were my friends:

"What's up Ell? Looks like you've seen a ghost!"

"I bloody-well have Bob."

"Hope it wasn't the nun," says he. *"You're supposed to die a year and a day after seeing her."*

Ah, cheers Bob!

After this helpful advice I made sure I forgot that date - on purpose, just in case suggestion does work.

I didn't think about it at the time but later it puzzled me that I had managed to catch up with my friends so quickly. Did something happen to me that I don't remember? Did I have *Added Time?* This area is a notorious hot-spot for otherworld encounters - from the nun to Roman soldiers, sprites and ghouls; these days it has Oxford United's horseshoe-shaped stadium plonked on it, and they are not doing well. Is it any wonder? Not to me.
Not yet

In 1977 I bought a mobile home in the middle of some flourishing ancient oak woods near the village of Radley not far from Oxford. I adored living there but for some pretty scary moments:

I was laying in bed reading and it was after 3 o'clock in the morning so I put down my magazine and switched off the light. Almost instantly I felt something sit on the end of my bed. Startled I opened my eyes and was about to sit up when a loud whirring and whooshing noise erupted and I could not move. The noise stopped and I could hear somebody walking backwards and forwards in the next room (kitchen). Whoever it was was talking but I couldn't quite hear what they were saying. The footsteps were similar to a woman walking on a solid floor in high heels but the mobile home floor was suspended wood. I wanted to leg it but I couldn't move so I did the only thing I could think of at the time . . . I prayed, and I prayed, and after what seemed like an age the whirring, whooshing noise returned and everything fell silent.

I lay awake until morning came. A slight odour of something burnt hung in the air. The first thing I did was knock up crosses from bits of wood and hung them all around the bedroom. For ages, when I went to bed, I'd even lay my socks on the floor in the shape of a cross. None of this did any good though.

A week or two later a friend asked me if I would do an Ouija with her. I hadn't touched it since my visit to the vicarage in 1973 and though I had a little trepidation I was starting to feel curious about it again. I told my workmate about it and he was really keen to give it a go so we arranged to meet up one night at her cottage on Old Boars Hill near Oxford. We laid out a circle of letters with a glass in the middle put our fingers on the glass and very quickly it began to move - much to the astonishment of my two friends. The first visitor was unintelligible; the second said he was the lady's brother who had passed several years ago. Some precise information was given and then suddenly the energy changed and the messages became increasingly unsettling and then threatening. We closed the table down straightaway. My workmate, a true (open-minded) sceptic, admitted afterwards that he tried to first hold down the glass and then push it but he couldn't succeed. After we had a coffee my friend drove me home. The nearer I got the more unsettled I felt . . . I just knew that I'd stirred something up.

Again I was reading in bed during the wee hours (hoping that daylight would come before anything else did) but I was so tired - I turned off the light . . . immediately I felt the pressure of something on the end of my bed. The whirring whooshing noise revved up like the last time . . . then stopped. I'm lying with my back to the door and I try to jump up but I can't move so I decide to feign sleep and, although it didn't seem to work last time, I pray. I'm immediately aware of a presence right behind me and I hear a voice. At the time it sounded like the most evil voice imaginable. It said:

"There he is. . .pretending to be asleep. . ."

And I was!

Then another similar sounding voice broke in: *"Shall we?"*

Can you imagine?

And the first voice replied: *"No. . .not yet!"*

I was praying and praying but it wasn't doing anything; and I was straining with all my might to move but I couldn't. I wasn't going to just lie there. I was formulating a plan . . . I'd leap up and lay into them before escaping out of the front door . . . but then I thought, 'I can't, I'm in the nick! I can't go running about in the middle of the night with no clothes on!' And then the whirring and whooshing started up again. Normality returned and I could move once more and there was the same burnt smell.

Stomach pain

I was still living in the mobile home but I'd met a new girlfriend and had started to divide my time between her parent's farm and my little home in the oak wood. We were in her mobile home on the farm when one morning, after vivid dreams that I remember involved whirlwinds and spinning buildings, I awoke with excruciating pain in my stomach - they reminded me of the intense pains I'd suffered when I had yellow jaundice but these were a bit higher. I hoped they'd go away but a few hours later they hadn't so my girlfriend drove me to the surgery in the nearby town.

The doctor examined me thoroughly but though my pains never let up he could not work out what the problem was. Fearing that I might have appendicitis he insisted that I go to hospital and said that he would call an ambulance immediately but my girlfriend said that she would drive me there. We went home to collect a few things and then drove to the John Radcliffe Hospital near Oxford. I was there for 3 days having tests but the pains had gone by the evening of the next day. Doctor's never found anything.

Electric silence

I was awoken in the early hours one night, by what I can't recall but immediately I could feel a presence and thought I could see a misty shape at the end of my bed; then I saw it move and the air felt electric, not sharp, sort of a gentle buzz; but it frightened me and I yelled out for it to go away, and it did. I fell back to sleep.

I was awoken early by a phone call. It was my brother. Sensing tears immediately I heard him say, *"Ell, I have some really sad new. Nan died last night."*

I still feel a twinge of guilt about this, my Nan had come to say goodbye and I'd told her to go away.

I've learnt though and now when I have visits from spirit - depending on the circumstances, due to me being a woos - I acknowledge them and anyway they have a very easy way about them now and they don't just jump out at me anymore - not for a while they haven't anyway. When spirits visit it is often when I'm actually with someone who is special to them and they just want me to let that person know that they are around. That can be a task.

Branded

On Saturday 13th April 1996 I awoke at about 7.30am, got up and went to the loo. When I got back into bed my partner suddenly threw back the covers and with a look of shock on her face, exclaimed, *"What is all that over your body?"*

I hadn't noticed anything. "Look!" she cried. On my right wrist were finger marks, long strangely shaped and configured; a geometric-like face on the left-hand side of my chest and a very strange claw or tail-like pattern on my left upper-arm, circles on my thighs and I was burnt red, like sunburn. All the marks/drawings appeared to be formed from blood being drawn to the surface of my skin; which was perfectly smooth with no indentation like sheet-marks leave. It was as if I'd been branded. My partner leapt out of bed to find her camera, came back a few minutes later and photographed the marks, which were fading fast by now. I'm often asked how long these marks lasted for but I don't know because I don't know what time they were made. My best guess, because most of my night-time experiences occur around four o'clock am, is that they remain on my skin for about four hours. It should also be noted that if my partner had not noticed the marks then we would never have known that they were there . . . but then, subsequent events suggest we were meant to acknowledge them . . . and photograph them.

Photos

A friend had all these photos checked out in Oxford University's skin and blood research laboratories. They could not explain them but they did say that they are not sheet-marks. The professor also said that when she looked at the finger mark photos (on page 99) she at first thought that I'd been gripping my arm for a long time - but then she realised I would have to have my hand on the opposite arms. I also went to a doctor in Australia who seemed really shaken by what was happening to me. After vainly searching her text books she sent me for a blood test and asked me to ring her in a couple of days. When I did the doctor wouldn't speak to me but the receptionist told me that the results of my blood test showed no problems.

I'm not 'O negative' or anything exotic; just your bog-standard 'O positive' but I have been told more than once during my encounters that nobody must have my blood. The first time I can remember was because I had decided to give blood one day in 1973 - which *they* said necessitated it being destroyed. That same night I suddenly fell very ill with crippling pain and the next day I was diagnosed with jaundice. The health visitor told me that they only just managed to get to my blood in time - smashed it, she said. Sounds over the top to me when I think about  it now but they must have had their reasons to destroy the container as well. Obviously hepatitis contaminated blood can be lethal if it is transfused into a vulnerable person.

The most obvious feature off this photograph is the face-like drawing but if you look there seems to be a definite pattern on the skin below it too. I reiterate the lines had no relief to them, my skin was perfectly smooth.

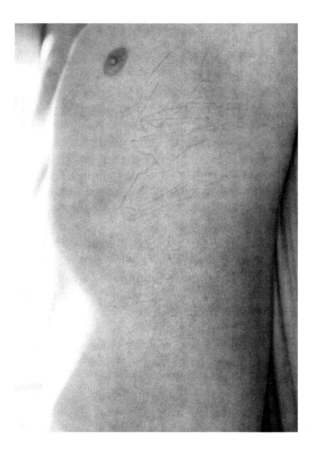

The next photo shows a really peculiar pattern on my left upper arm. I'm at a loss as to what it is; could it be some kind of hand or paw but then this is *otherworld* stuff and maybe there is nothing we can compare it with on this plane(t). If anyone knows what it could be then please write and tell me.

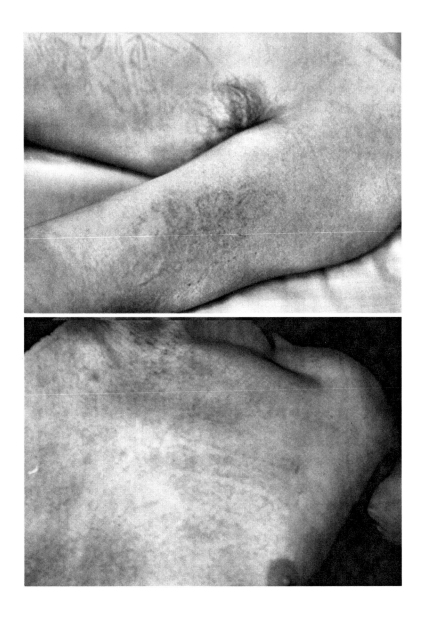

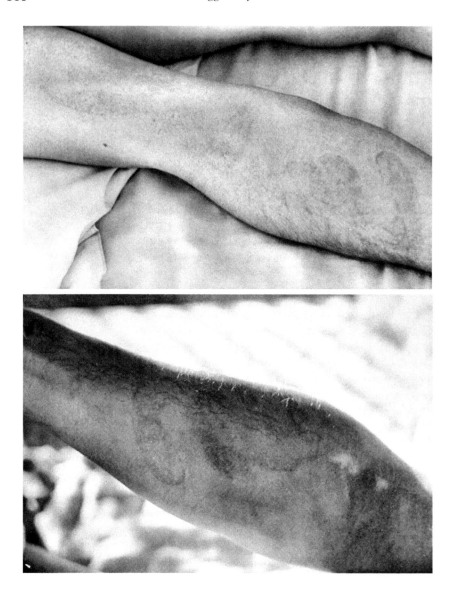

Well, that was it, *on for young and old* from here on, for weeks, nearly every night and sometimes during the day the visitors came. But that first morning my partner was at her wits end, absolutely terrified. I tried to calm her but I had no easy explanation for it other than vague recollections that it might be something to do with alien abduction . . . and then I remembered the UFO group that I'd looked up in the telephone directory a few weeks before. I rang the number and spoke to a man who assured me that there was nothing to worry about and that abductions don't occur more than once. He advised me to make notes of everything we could remember and I told him that my partner had photographed the marks. *"Good,"* he said. *"We have a meeting this Friday coming at Murdoch University; could you bring them along to show us?"* I asked the man if there would be anyone there who could help my partner, or anyone who knew something about these things, but he didn't think so. I told the man that if I could I would attend their meeting and he said to phone him anytime if I needed to. He was a good bloke but the society didn't seem as if it would be of any help for my partner. For some reason I wasn't scared - except when I went to bed and at the point of being taken . . . "Peace, no harm", they'd say and later, "We do not understand your fear."

Well, as I said, every night almost we'd have a visit. My partner saw more than I did of my abductions, she's a gutsy little thing and she'd cling on to me with her arms, even her legs, attempting to stop them. One time it took a sharp jab in the knee of something to make her loosen her grip which left a big blister. She was herself launched through 3 walls, she counted them. My girlfriend has provided accounts of her own testimony which are included further on in this book.

The alarming activity accelerated as the week progressed and my girlfriend's terror increased; still I didn't know where to turn. Whoever or whatever it was had a purpose. I'd wake up burnt, feeling sick, usually with strange finger marks and patterns but otherwise ok, my concern was for my partner.

In midweek I went to my night school class where I told my close friend about what was happening and showed her the photos my girlfriend had taken. The next day she phoned me, *"I have a good friend who is a counsellor and I've spoken to her. She is very open-minded and if* (my girlfriend) *likes, she will talk with her. You can meet her at my place if you prefer?"*

I think it was on the Thursday that I first met Mary Rodwell and showed her my photos. We've been good mates ever since. Mary offered to visit us on the following Saturday morning but meantime I had a meeting to attend at Murdoch.

On Friday 19th April, at midday, I had an urge to meditate. I lay down on the bed closed my eyes and immediately felt a chill. Something cold wrapped around my ankles and I felt hands pushing down on my shoulders. Something whizzed around inside my mouth but I never even tried to open my eyes.

That evening I drove to Murdoch University alone. My partner wasn't ready to talk to anyone about it but I promised to find out what I could.

After a very entertaining lecture by the president of the society, Professor John Frodsham we retired for coffee and biscuits. I met the man who I'd talked to on the phone and he introduced me to other members. Near the end of the meeting I was conversing with one of the committee members, the late Simon Harvey-Wilson, when my right earlobe began to itch like mad. One of the few things about Australia that really annoy me is mozzies!

I left the meeting having found that although it was brimming with knowledgeable people there really was'nt anyone who could help my partner. Disappointed and with an ear itching like billy-o I walked into the kitchen and told my partner all about the evening. "My flippin' ear is driving me mad," I grumbled to my partner; "Have I been bitten by a mozzie?"

As I stood under the light she bent back my earlobe and with a gasp of 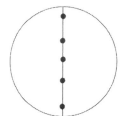 surprise she said, *"No, it isn't a mozzie bite! It's been cut, like surgery. There's a fine straight cut with 5 dots that seem to be holding the edges of the cut together and it's all in a circle."*

I asked my girlfriend to draw what she could see. (Left)

This was quite strange because over the previous couple of weeks I had been feeling something tiny, about the size of a grain of sand, in this earlobe. Now it was gone and I had what looked like scars from an operation!

My partner took a couple of photographs; we had a hot drink, and then retired to bed.

The next morning Mary came around as arranged. We told her about the events since I'd first met her and showed her my ear. Mary, who is a trained nurse, suggested that it looked like the result of micro-surgery. Outside, in the sun, we took another photograph. My ear had stopped itching now.

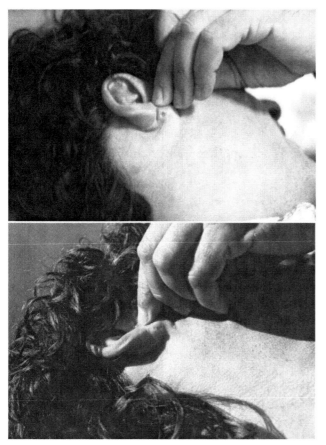

This was only the beginning. Over the next few weeks *contact* accelerated so much so that the whole house seemed to vibrate with a subtle, yet intense energy. All sorts of other strange things occurred besides what I have reported already. It was a huge challenge to keep focussed on everyday life and responsibilities when at any time, day or night, I could find myself being whipped away to who knows where.

Sometimes I did recognise where I was so I would realise that I must have been there before. I was taken down into tunnels and up into space. I walked around huge, usually empty, vividly bright rooms and saw massive white storage units which opened with red stick handles. I was shown small life-forms growing in tubes, body parts - legs, arms, feet and hands etc - in containers and told that they were used in 1939. I was shown disasters, destroyed cities black and smoking; and occasionally a disc-shaped UFO would fly over the scene.

I have memories of being on crafts but as with much of this experience my memories are vague and sketchy. I've had the floated out through the walls or windows thing as well but sometimes I don't remember how I got out. I've been carried aboard drawn up in a light and at other times I just remember being somewhere one moment and on board the next. As for take off the means of exits seem to be just as varied. It might just zoom off or it can rise very steadily until it gets to a certain point above the Earth and then they're *outa here*. At other times the craft jumps in quick spurts and leaves a pale-mustardy-brown smoky ring which you can see because the craft becomes transparent.

Aboard crafts I've seen small bald and naked beings that busy themselves around consoles. Their skin is the colour of ripened wheat, they have almond-shaped eyes, two tiny holes instead of a nose, small mouths which are tight and motionless slits, impossibly thin necks; the tops of their heads rise to a hump at the back. As far as I can recall they always ignore me. I have seen other beings too some are very human-looking, they're blond mostly but not always. When these types come near me I feel like I am fizzing. They're quite aloof generally but I have come across some that are gregarious. I've seen some horrible looking creatures too, so horrible that I can't bring myself to even think about them. It's as if I mustn't think about them.

There is however one special being who always has much to say to me. When I say 'say' he doesn't actually talk he communicates by telepathy though sometimes he does make his speech audible externally. He looks extremely ancient, rather similar to the other small creatures but his skin is covered in folds and he wears a white gown with a hood -

which is rarely over his head. He seems very wise. He can also change his appearance at a whim into anything he wants. One recollection is standing on board a craft facing him. I had a white gown on and he was telling me something that was important judging by the sternness of his demeanour. All I could think at this crucial moment was, 'How does that skinny little neck hold up that great big head.' I was like that at school here too - always daydreaming instead of paying attention.

Some excerpted diary entries from 1996:

Saturday 13th April

Woke up about 7.30am. Felt a bit groggy as I went to the loo. Got back into bed and suddenly *my partner* flung the covers off me and shouted, "What's all those marks all over you?"

Sunday 14th April

During the night *my partner* found my lapis lazuli stone behind my back and put it under my pillow.

Tuesday 16th April

Awoke in the morning about 7am, more red marks but they seem different, I'm not sure how. I feel burnt on the left side of my face and inside my left thigh. It feels like sunburn. I'd had a very restless night. *My partner* said I was tossing and turning all night and whimpering. Took photos.

During the day the burning sensation spread all over my body, it wasn't very red but felt like sunburn to touch.

Wednesday 17th April

When I awoke I knew they had been again. I couldn't see any red marks but I remember being moved around in my sleep.

I hadn't got much sleep. I was aware they were with me but I was in a half sleep sort of trance. I felt the soreness going.

In the night I got up to go to the loo twice. The first time the living room light was on - I remember clearly turning it off before going to bed.

Amongst other things I saw in the night were symbols - but I couldn't remember them when I woke up even though I tried.

I was told, *"Stevie Wonder is not the person I think he is."*

Thursday 18th April

The one thing I remember from last night is being told: *"Peace, no harm."*

Friday 19th April

In the night someone spoke to me, *"The visitors mean no harm. They are friendly and have a beautiful philosophy."*

My partner's elder daughter has awoken with a passion for ancient Egypt and wants her bedroom decorated like it.

I meditated at midday. Immediately I had a message, *"Settle down and wait for the advance party. You have important tasks to accomplish."* I was on a table in their craft. I saw brief glimpses of one being behind me and then felt hands pressing down on my shoulders. Something cold was holding my feet down. There was something or some sort of energy inside my mouth; it was wobbly and vibrating around especially on the left side of my mouth. It was very fast and pulsating.

When I came out I felt pressure on my upper arms. They were aching as if I'd been doing lots of hard physical work. I was told, *"There is an important group to meet."*

Saw a flame coloured beam of light shine down to the south (very quick). Went to UFORM meeting at Murdoch University. Speaker apologised for starting late but my watch said 7.30pm. While there my right earlobe felt itchy. I scratched it and there was something there.

When I arrived home I asked *my partner* to look at my earlobe. (see report page 119)

Saturday 20th April

My face has gone red all around my mouth, brow and nose, also sideburn area is peeling and itchy. I have been itching for days.

Mary Rodwell came round today and spoke with *my partner*. I think it helped. I told Mary about my visit to the UFORM meeting at Murdoch University. She said she might go there herself one day. We showed Mary my ear and photographed it again. It looks as if it has healed quite a bit since last night which seems odd.

Found out that my watch had lost 10 minutes - remembered thinking it was strange the news starting at 5.50pm instead of 6pm. It's never been wrong before.

Sunday 21st April

I was taken down a circular tunnel through rock. We were going along a kind of railway track.

Woke up 8.30am. Large round circle on my right thigh but it faded fast. Took a photo. Took 2 more photos of my ear.

Monday 22nd April

Today I was regressed by Mary Rodwell. I went back to my childhood and saw myself watching a tall dark figure watching me. He was standing in front of something extremely bright and golden.

Then saw myself being carried by two people in white (head and body). The men carried me backwards with one arm each. Then saw myself sitting on a table with 2 men in white to my right and others milling about. They were talking to each other. The room was very bright. I already had some recollections of these things.

Tuesday 23rd April
I am told, *"Susan touched the stone."*
I am shown a brown, old-fashioned looking van racing along a dirt track. It tries to turn and rolls over. A turquoise lake, a fence going into the water.
I see white buildings with square flat tops near the sea.
I went to Mary's house for a psychic evening.

Wednesday 24th April
Meditated in the morning.
I was shown a huge army standing in the shape of a 5-pointed star; they had no weapons. Next the vision of a lion running amongst the stars. Next I was shown Clinton and Yeltsin walking down some stairs.
Saw huge tidal waves and humungous rocks coming out of the sea, explosions, the tidal waves were 100s of feet high.
Felt very tired and exhausted.
Had a shower and noticed red marks all over my body. Took photographs but couldn't focus properly (photographs not too good) I feel like I've been run over by an express train again. Don't remember anything about *aliens* touching me. Saw a body on a bed, it was white. I was told: *"The body parts were all used in 1939".* I had seen human body parts in drawers.

Thursday 25th April
I awoke and found finger marks on my chest. I took photographs. My lapis lazuli stone was on the side table after I had double checked last night to see it was under my pillow before going to sleep.
During the evening my chest - over my heart area - is very tender and feels strange to touch. I asked to be healed during the night.

Friday 26th April
Lots of marks over my body this morning - a red circle over my heart and a line straight down the centre of my chest, and another red circle over my right thigh. This was over a scar that *my partner* noticed but I don't remember how I got. The area of my nose and right side of my face feels burnt. My back feels burnt and also my abdomen. I have diarrhoea. I have now had this off and on for about 3 weeks. I am sore around my groin area too.
My partner says she watched an oddly behaving light over my face during the night. She seems to have lost much of her fear.
I am still being shown warships at sea in the night.

27th April

A nightmare last night. Dreamt I was shown body parts assembled into beings, some human like, others humanoid. Awoke screaming a warning. Strangely *my partner* didn't wake though. I think I woke in a different place.

Marks on me again but they disappeared exceptionally fast - this time circles on thigh and side of my body; finger marks arms and chest. Only managed one photograph.

I must have been told I was going somewhere that concerned me because I remember asking my guide to protect me.

The beings I saw this time seemed lifeless.

My nose is blocked up this morning. I feel strange, frightened and apprehensive.

Friday 3rd May

Today I had a flashback to my childhood. Lots of *aliens* - like the little ones I described - were all around me. I was lying on a bed. I was very young.

I am having red marks regularly but no one seems interested. I'm even losing interest myself.

Saturday 4th May

During meditation I got very hot and itchy. I saw lots but couldn't hang on to any of it. Came round burnt and feeling on edge.

Monday 6th May

Vision of a young blond haired woman, in a white coat, standing with hands in her coat pockets, looks cold. It is dark, night time. She is standing near a telephone box near a junction, the; pavement is very wide. A light-blue small station-wagon type vehicle pulls up. The passenger door opens. The driver, a man, is talking to the girl - possibly offering her a lift? He has white hair and beard (glasses too I think). She gets in. the seat covers are lambskin. As they are driving I can see some cranes and derricks in front of them in the distance - I think it is docks, so probably Fremantle. There is something in the passenger-side foot well of the car - could be a bag. (See pages 95, 96, 155)

Fremantle from Cottesloe Groyne. It is uncannily similar to the visionary scene I saw.

Wednesday 8th May

I may have found a spot where craft could have landed, in the corner of the front garden - the leaves etc are scorched but there is no reason that they should be.

Thursday 9th May

I woke up at about 4.30am with marks on my shoulder - some sort of design - and finger marks on the right of my chest.
Later I went out to the place I found yesterday and there was a strong smell of something chemical.

Friday 10th May

I had a repetition of the same vision I had on Monday this time I was shown that the driver of the car was wearing a priest's collar.
These visions almost certainly apply to the abduction of Sarah Spiers from the corner of Stirling Highway and Stirling Road on 27th January 1996. (See above and pages 95, 96, 155)

Saturday 11th May

I felt they were coming again last night and they did. I don't have much recollection of what happened but I heard lots of strange noises - *my partner* was taken. She said that she was launched through 3 walls.

Tuesday 14th May

When meditating this afternoon I felt great pressure around my head and a beautiful warmth rise up my body from my feet.

My partner saw the gold coloured Porsche parked outside our house again today, the driver of which had spooked her a few weeks back.

Last Night

What I think was the last visitation of this March to May 1996 sequence occurred after I had decided to myself that I was going to remain fully conscious throughout the entire experience. I wanted to know everything about what went on and if possible bring something back. I thought about it all day.

We retired to bed, around midnight I think it was, and soon fell asleep. At some point during the night I had a nightmare and called out waking my partner who asked me what was wrong. I related the whole tale to her . . . how I had been cycling along this narrow country road that I remembered from my childhood - between the villages of Chislehampton and Clifton Hampden. Without even making any attempt to stop I rode straight through some trees on thw side of the road and into a pond . . . down, down, down I went . . . and I couldn't get of the bikes, no matter how much I tried. It was at this point I think I must have yelled out.

(As I write this I've remembered and realised something . . . because of this nightmare I went to visit this place when I went back to Oxfordshire again. I couldn't remember a pond being anywhere along the road but I did recollect the location and the clump of trees, on a bend near some buildings. Well, there was a pond behind the trees, but not deep however there are some pretty military-like buildings very close by, and this isn't very far away at all from where I spotted the crop circle. I wonder, might there be an underground facility here?)

My partner seemed to listen then assured me that everything was ok and fell back to sleep . . . but something didn't seem right about her behaviour it was as if she was asleep when she was talking to me. I lay on my back for a little while wondering whether *they* were coming and eventually I closed my eyes again, laid on my right side and tried to doze off. Almost immediately I felt the energy in the room change, it felt electric, on edge, everything was intensely quiet . . . and waiting . . .

Although my eyes were closed I could sense the sudden presence of other beings in the room beside my girlfriend and me. It was then that I felt something plop onto the bed between her and me, near my waist. Somehow I knew there was another one to the left side of me and one more at the end of the bed. On the other side of the bed from me we had a large built-in wardrobe with mirrored doors and I squinted my eyes to look into the glass. As I peered through the darkness I could see a willowy, thin whitish-grey misty being waving his long arms over me. It was in the process of solidifying and I wondered whether it would eventually turn into one of the preoccupied little beings I'd seen on the crafts but they weren't the same. This one was much more supple and lively.

I found myself with my eyes closed again and then something took hold of my right elbow. The touch was light but firm and it felt to me like the skin of a dolphin might feel. There was no physical force at all but something was making me sit up. As I steadily rose I repeated over and over again, "I'm going to go, I'm going to go, I am not frightened, I'm going to go, I will remember everything." . . . and I was sitting upright . . . and I panicked, calling out for my partner . . . and then I was laying back down gently and my girlfriend was asking, *"What's up love?"*

"They've been again, they've been again!" I blurted out; and all she said was, *"No they haven't darling,"* and fell asleep again.

I lay there filled with thoughts of regret and fear and frustration and confusion . . . I'd asked them to come and I'd virtually told them that I would overcome my fear but I hadn't. I felt despondent. I didn't sleep much that night. Eventually dawn and the magpies of the morning broke and not long after I heard my partner say, *"Good morning love, can't you sleep?"*

I told her that I'd been trying but though I felt really tired I just couldn't.

"They did come," I said.

"Who did?" she responded.

"The visitors, aliens, whatever they are," I said, "They did come . . . look!" and I showed her the finger marks and other patterns on my skin.

"When did you tell me?" she asked, *"I was asleep."*

"No, you woke up and I told you then and you just said they hadn't and fell back to sleep. I told you about the nightmare I had before that too. Do you remember?"

She didn't and I truly think that I was taken that night and that somehow they caused her to communicate with me as if she were awake. I remembered how I thought at the time that she was not behaving as she normally would.

In time I think I've begun to understand why I'd *bottled it* at the point of going when I'd prepared myself so determinedly to go. I'm the sort of person who once I've made my mind up to do something I'll do it come hell or high water. Perhaps it was sheer terror but when I replay the event again the beings that came were not who I expected. As I watched that being materialise out of nowhere and into something I did not recognise then I think I can be less hard on myself for changing my mind. After all who were they? If it had been my little friend then I'd have had little fear, maybe none.

Some of the (often bizarre) things they say.

"Stevie wonder is not who you think he is."

"People go round saying 'Napoleon did this, Napoleon did that; but what about the golden shilling?"

"Peace. . .No harm."

"The supreme leader is not Henkler (or Hinkler) but Bob Brown."

"The body parts were all used in 1939."

The Morrigan

A number of years ago Mary called me to say that a woman had been in touch and wanted to speak to me about my experiences. The woman was accompanied by a man and another woman. Also present were Mary, J. (a female psychic friend who does attachment release), and me. I was late arriving but from the instant I got there until the moment they went this woman attacked me psychically and never took her eyes off me once. I had sensed her darkness as soon as I had arrived and put up a psychic shield. Hovering in the ether between me and her was the object she was looking for, had been sent to find - an object that looked a cross between something Arthurian and Star Wars I thought at the time. After an intense time the woman gave up and all three of them made to go. She  said to me she would come back and that she hadn't finished yet; immediately I knew what I had to say to keep her away. I repeated the words exactly and I haven't seen her since.

Mary and J. could see what had been going on and when I came back into the consulting room they said how uneasy they had been. Something that stood out for me was that none of the three visitors had a soul, empty shells motivated by a non-human force. I see this increasingly these days especially celebrities and politicians, people like that - with a bit of clout.

Plane sight

One night, in early October 1997, I was driving alone along the A40 road towards Oxford from Witney. It was between 10pm and 11pm the sky was clear and very dark. I wasn't very far out of Witney, coming down the hill, when I saw an aeroplane in the sky, to the east over the village of  Eynsham, between myself and Oxford. The plane was about the size of a small airliner and it had no lights on at all. As I got closer to Eynsham I realised that it was not moving. I could see the craft at all times except for when it as obscured by a stand of tall trees. When I reached Eynsham I slowed right down and unwound the car's window to have a good look at it. It was as silent as it was stationary; just hanging there over the village close to the road but much lower than you'd think. I gauged the height of it roughly from the trees nearby - about 3 times the height.. It was a solid thing with its nose pointing north towards the road. I didn't stop, I didn't even take a photograph - though I had one in the car - I just carried on. As I drove away I kept an eye on it in the rear view mirror and wing mirror and it didn't move, just hung there as if it was frozen in the sky.

The incident played on my mind all night and I tried to rationalise what it could have been. The only possibility I could think of was that it might have been an elaborately authentic-looking balloon tethered to the ground for some event in the village. I didn't see any tethers and the plane didn't sway at all (which blimps do), and it didn't look like anything other than an aeroplane in every way but it seemed the only alternative to a *extraordinary* event. In the morning I phoned the Eynsham post office and asked if there was any special event going on in Eynsham? There wasn't. I asked if there had been a giant blimp over the village within the last few days. There hadn't been. A friend of mine drove to Eynsham to have a look for me but there was nothing there. How I wish I'd stopped, got out and photographed it but it's really strange how often people see such strange things and then inexplicably don't think to photograph them.

"Really enjoyed your talk mate; it takes guts to tell it like it is these days."

I turned to see a man in his thirties wearing a red shirt and a cheery smile. He held out his hand and introduced himself: *"I'm Dennis"* he beamed, *"Pleased to meet you."*

"Ellis Taylor", I replied, "Likewise."

Dennis had large hands and carried the look of a rugby player; a confident man with an open, cheerful face and an Essex accent.

This exchange occurred during the final break of the October 2007 Cornish UFO conference, just outside the lecture theatre in Truro College.

I'd noticed Dennis in the audience while I gave my presentation. He had stood out. (Sometimes a person's aura will have an extra sheen to it, which usually signifies to me that in some way I have, or will have, a connection with them.) We chatted for a while and I asked him whether he had had any supernatural experiences because it was obvious that he had - Well, it was to me, but perhaps not to most anyone else for he seemed a really conventional, everyday, down-to-earth bloke - a lorry driver by way of a crust.

It turned out that he and his daughter had a terrifying experience where they were chased by a UFO after inadvertently coming across what sounded to me like a landed craft in a field near to a small town on the north Cornish coast. I'll do my best to recall what he told me:

It was graveyard dark as they slipped between the stone walls and hedges of the twisting narrow lanes of country Cornwall when all of a sudden; at the top of a rise they peered down to see lights, constructions, vehicles . . . and *'people'* scurrying about where there should have been just a pasture.

Dennis stopped the car trying to make sense of what was happening but that minute or so was enough, long enough for their car to be noticed. Dennis, instinctively aware that he had stumbled upon something he was not supposed to see, floored the accelerator and with his heart pumping burnt for the sanctuary of civilisation. Immediately a craft, with blinking lights, appeared to the side of them spinning in the misty air no higher than the trees. First to the left and then to the right of them the UFO kept pace. Dennis tried desperately not to panic his young daughter but the look on her dad's face betrayed his anxiety. "Daddy, daddy," she cried. "What is it?" "Make it go . . . Make it go!"

"We're nearly home sweetheart." Dennis somehow mustered the calmness from somewhere.

After what seemed like forever the car carrying Dennis and his daughter swerved into the main street of the town. Looking round there was no sign of the UFO and Dennis breathed a sigh of relief. The streets were deserted. It was late, very late and Dennis turned his car for home, at least he started to because in the confusion of what had just occurred he realised that he didn't know the way home; but by a stroke of good fortune he noticed two men a little way down the street who he took to be fishermen. Pulling up beside them he wound the car window down. "Excuse me," he said . . . "Sorry to bother you; but are you from round here?" They replied in the affirmative and said that they were just on their way to work; whereupon Dennis asked them directions.

"The men seemed odd," he told me, *"distant, weird, and sort of pasty-faced. . .One of them pulled out a roadmap and then they both began to pore over it."*

Dennis couldn't help thinking how strange it was that two local people would need to look at a roadmap to give him directions to somewhere close by never mind have one on them in the first place . . .

"I'm just about to start my talk now", said a voice behind me. It was Dave Gillham, president of the Cornwall UFO Group and organiser of the conference.

"Have you reported all this to Dave (Gillham)?" I asked. Dennis said he had.

Several aspects of Dennis's account lead me to suspect that much more occurred to him – and, if so, possibly his daughter as well - on that night. For this reason I asked Dennis whether he had ever been regressed.

"No, I haven't, but I really think I'd like to now," Dennis answered. *"The incident has disturbed me ever since it happened."*

"I'll introduce you to Dave Coggins, if you like", I offered.

David Coggins is a hypnotist and regressionist from south Wales; he'd stepped in, at the last minute, to speak at the Cornwall conference after an American speaker had pulled out just before the gun.

When the conference had finished I introduced Dennis to David Coggins. Hopefully Dennis will be able to discover what exactly happened to him on that terrifying night.

I'd arranged to meet up with my friend David Gillham the next morning (Monday) for what has become for us, a traditional after-conference jaunt around sacred sites in Cornwall. We hadn't decided where we were going but I had awoken with a desire, more an insistent urge, to visit St Nectan's Glen. It seemed a lifetime ago that I last trod the sacred path along the little Trevillet River through the glen to the healing waters that spill so joyously over the ancient kieve. Dave had never been there before so he was well up for the trip. Before long we were clipping northwards along the A30. [44]

For a reason I can't explain I took an early turning, which meant that we went the long way to St Nectan's, through Tintagel. When I reached the junction with the main road opposite King Arthur's Hall, in the centre of town, I should have turned right but instead turned left. I did wonder what was going on but I didn't dwell on it. Only in hindsight can one make some sense of these things. [45]

I drove through Tintagel past the shops and the footpath to Tintagel Castle not thinking where I was going. Something invisible was driving us.

View of Tintagel Castle from the hotel.

Now, I've been to Tintagel many times and I know it quite well. I've seen most of what there is to see; but up till now I had never ventured into the Castle Hotel grounds. This time though I drove straight in. 'Why did I do this?' I tried not to show my discomfort to Dave but it was becoming more and more difficult not to. After parking the car at the front of the hotel

[44] www.stnectan.currantbun.com
[45] King Arthur's Hall, www.kingarthursgreathalls.com/page%202.htm

we headed for a better view of the timeless scenery from the cliff edges. The opposite headland bears Tintagel Castle moulded to the contours of the rocky outland and island. Tintagel Castle is the mythological birthplace of King Arthur, and below this, carved into the cliffs at sea level, Merlin's Cave. We took some photos before the batteries in Dave's camera expired.[46]

Personally I find the Castle Hotel building a pug-ugly carbuncle but *each to their own*. It was built during the last breath of Victoria's reign in one of the most indescribably beautiful settings in all of Albion. Sometimes I've wondered, during quiet ozone moments, why Merlin hasn't launched a thunderbolt at it . . .

Anyway . . . a note on a front window pane of the hotel said the joint was open to non-residents. "Let's go inside," says Dave excitedly. Dave seems much more impressed than me. "We could have a coffee," I muttered. So we ventured in. I found the interior a bit naff. I suspected that a Peckham lad in a rust-bucket, yellow Reliant Regal had made a killing here. Pink and red fabrics, furniture, and carpets loitered in the background spiked by fake swords and tacky axes. I ordered two cappuccinos from the dead-eyed waitress in the sharply pressed uniform.

Still feeling uneasy and careful to avoid standing under any chandeliers I rehearsed the immortal (misquoted) line under my breath just in case . . . "Get yer coat Trig we're going".[47]

While we waited for our coffee I was having a *sticky-beak* into the adjoining rooms that were decorated in much the same way, when I felt a wave of cold air coming at me from behind me. I turned to see a bald-headed man with a haunted expression that I felt concealed a well of suppressed intensity, or was it anger? He smiled and said, *"Hello, I'm Ted Stourton, one of the owners. I'm sorry I can't stop but we are undergoing*

---

[46] Tintagel Castle, www.tintagelweb.co.uk/Tintagel%20Castle.htm
[47] Really, "Drink up. We're going." Only Fools and Horses ~ Yuppie Love: www.geocities.com/hookyscripts/Episode_41.htm
With apologies to John Sullivan, http://en.wikipedia.org/wiki/John_Sullivan_%28writer%29

renovations at the moment; please feel free to look around and take photographs if you wish." He then turned and breezed out.

Dave and I wandered around the large Victorian-style dining room-cum-lounge with its faux round table and very impressive views of the cliffs and sea – at all times it felt like we were being watched. Creepy wasn't in it! Around the walls were paintings and drawings, and photographs of famous people with Mr Stourton and others with another man who I assume was one of the other owners. There were photographs of British and U.S. stage, film, TV and music stars of past and present eras; Isaac Hayes, Cary Grant – I can't remember who else except there is a drawing of Billy Connolly that could be a self-portrait, together with some words from the *Jedi-jester.* Then - just as I was about to read the *Big Yin's* scribble - enter stage right Mr Stourton. . .*"Have you seen* the Light-box,*"* he inquires.

"Uhhhh ? . . . "

"What do you do?" he asks Dave, while fixing him with an intense stare which causes Dave to feel uncomfortable. I don't know why but I sensed that this was some kind of mind game being attempted, so I interrupted. Ted centred himself and took aim at me,

"And, what do you do..."

"I write and paint," says I.

Ted, doubled his efforts . . . *"You are an artist then!"*

"I paint houses, but I used to work as a decorative artist yes."

Assuming that all was not lost he invited us to follow him. Well, we were up for an adventure so we thought *why not!* On the way we passed a smartly-uniformed male member of staff who acknowledged us with a shadow-eyed, but smiling mouthed visage.

Mr Stourton took us into an untidy office where he said to take a seat. Sitting with him around his desk he reached for a pad of paper and a pen and turned to Dave," *What is it that is destroying your life at the moment?"*

'That's a conversation stopper!' I thought.

Dave didn't know what to say to that so he gave up and turned to me asking the same question. With the benefit of forewarning I was able to give him a half-respectable answer and told him that I was in control of my own life. Ted dropped the pen (with not a mere hint of exasperation), stood up, and urged us to follow him. He opened a door and led us down some steps into the cellar. The cellar comprised of numerous small cell-like rooms, with and without doors, which he called studios.

"I've helped thousands of artists," boasted Ted; they apply to us and if we accept them we allow them to use a studio here for a week, free of charge."

(I'd heard of this place before. The owner of a bookshop in Glastonbury had mentioned it to me years ago. He'd told me that he knew of artists, musicians and writers from Glastonbury and elsewhere, who had stayed at the hotel.)

Ted took Dave and me along a passageway to a room at the end. The room was painted white with a design at dado-rail height and against one wall a tidy selection of paint pots and brushes with other artists' materials. Against another wall to the right were some old dining chairs. In the middle of the room stood another dining chair with an acoustic guitar leaning against it. Beckoning us to sit down on two chairs by the wall Ted picked up the guitar and sat down in the centre of the room and began to sing and play Donovan's, "Catch the Wind".[48]

Dave excitedly nudging me, and with a beaming smile, he chuckled, *"We get up to some stuff, don't we Ell?" Cor, bloody 'ell nobody would believe it all, would they?"*

Ted sang and played beautifully undoubtedly enhanced by the superb acoustics this room offered - but yet something was distracting me. I could hear a woman sobbing and I began to feel her tears, tears of hopelessness and her feelings of despair a sense of being trapped. She was a young woman, wearing a hat and a long dress of the Edwardian period; she sat opposite Ted and facing in his direction. I closed my eyes

---

[48] http://uk.youtube.com/watch?v=h2arEUEAWck

attempting to focus in on the spirit of this lady when I heard a rustle next to me, at which, without missing a beat, Ted said, "Please don't take photos . . . " Another rustle and the only sounds I could hear were Ted and the guitar. The sound of the sobbing was gone but the plaintive atmosphere remained.

When Ted finished his haunting song he stood up, replaced the guitar, and again said he was going to show us the *Light-box*. Dave was understandably quite overcome by the experience and enthused to Ted about it. Ted didn't flinch from his dead-eye stare.

"There's a woman crying in here," I said to Ted. "She sobbed through nearly all the song."

"Oh, that was the woman last night," he replied. "She kept crying."

We retraced our footsteps down the passage, past empty studios to a room at the end where Ted again motioned for us to sit down.

"Take a seat. . .Any one," he said removing some tissues from a window sill, *"She's left her tissues in here too!"*

This time there were three chairs against the back wall. Ted turned on a switch and then walked over to a stack of rolled-up canvasses and chose one. Returning to the wall opposite us he unravelled the canvass and held it up so that a light shone through it. The painting had an intriguing effect. Dave loved it but it made me feel sick. Ted showed us a few more of the paintings - which evoked similar responses in both of us - and then said to Dave, *"Which one do you like best?"* Dave replied that he liked the first one. Ted held the said painting to the light again. *"For a painting like this I would charge 10 to 20 thousand pounds,"* he said; *"But you can have it for £320."* He didn't even blink . . . Dave couldn't stop! - He was also speechless, which, for anyone who knows Dave, is no common thing.

Again, I had the benefit of seeing what was coming.

"And which one did you like best," came Ted's predictable next move.

"Oh, I don't know . . . perhaps the second one," I answered.

"This one," says Ted, holding up a mite smaller painting to the light.

"Yes," says I.

"Well, this one would usually be about the same price – 10 to 20 thousand, maybe 15 thousand; but you can have it for. . .£290," he generously offered.

"No, I'd never buy anything for £290," I said, "I don't like the number. It has ominous potential."

Facially Ted's expression was surprised but his eyes changed not a jot. *"Well, what about 180?"* he countered.

"Nuh, I don't like it and neither of us came here to buy a painting. Thanks anyway."

At this Ted rolled up his wares and announced that he had to get back to work; so, off we went, back up the stairs where we landed in the reception. The same male staff-member as before came through another door at the same moment but this time he was devoid of both glint and smile. Ted disappeared through another door and returned almost immediately on the end of two leads pulled by two lunging **dogs**. They crashed through the opposite door into a room and I followed - I've no idea why. As the door was shutting I suddenly realised that the man with the dogs wasn't Ted – weird!

Stepping back into the reception I noticed a cluster of *soul-less* staff in the reception office staring at Dave and me. *"Let's finish our coffee,"* says Dave. I'd forgotten about our coffee. "I'll be with you in a moment mate," I said, "I need to visit the loo first."

When I got back to the lounge I noticed Dave was staring intently at something on a table. *"We've just said no to billions!"* he gasped. *"Look at this!"*

Dave passed me a newspaper. On the front page a headline stated something like, "The World's Billionaires Gather For a Sale of Paintings by the World's Greatest Living Artist." and "Ted Stourton's Paintings Will Sell for Millions" For a Sale of Paintings by the World's Greatest Living Artist." Underneath it had a photograph of Mr Stourton and a collection of his nauseous paintings.[49]

---

[49] The newspaper has been updated from the copy we saw but it says basically the same thing: www.londonlocals.co.uk/Online%20edition.html

Although the newspaper was titled, "Independent" and the rest of the paper seemed *kosher* I didn't believe it was real. Dave grabbed a copy anyway and we made our escape . . . er sorry . . . we left.

In the car park Dave asked me if I was all right. I told him I was. He said that I had changed in some way when we were in the hotel. I said that I just felt that we were in the presence of something 'not of this world' - beings without souls - aliens of some sort perhaps. I had felt as if I needed to be *on the case* for both our sakes. That it felt to me like one of those 60s TV shows where someone unwittingly drives into a small country town that turns out to be taken over by aliens.

Sacred waters

At last we were on our way to where we were supposed to be going, St. Nectan's Glen, a place of stunning beauty and sanctity between Tintagel and Boscastle.[50]

I have had some wonderful, unforgettable moments there over the years. In the late 1990s I journeyed to St. Nectan's Glen; I think it was for the second time. I clambered up on the ledge overlooking the basin sat for a while and then took a photograph before climbing down to the bottom. I was all alone and such an urge to meditate in this exquisitely beautiful place came upon me. Afterwards I took three quick-fire successive photographs of the waterfall (with my 35m film camera). - See opposite.

---

[50] St. Nectan's Glen: www.ellisctaylor.com/stnectansglen.html
   St. Nectan's Glen www.tintagelweb.co.uk/St%20Nectan's%20Glen.htm

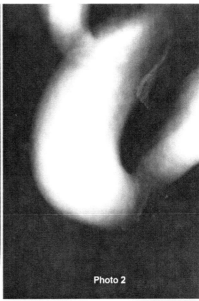

ST. NECTAN'S WATERFALL & KIEVE after meditation

This serpent-like weaving *something* seems to have used the energy of this place to manifest.

Photo 1. Shows something, extremely bright, just visible in the bottom right corner.

Photo 2. While the water is still visible in the background the rest of the scene has vanished. Could this be saying something to us about the properties of water?

Photo 3. Only the strange energy form remains

The composition of these energy-forms at St. Nectan's waterfall reminded me of something:

During a New Year's Eve party 1996/97, I think it was, someone had taken a photograph using my camera. When the film was developed a huge white-coil dominated the scene and I assumed that there was a fault with the developing or something. Seems I was wrong.

Remote views

We also visited Rocky Valley across the road, where a few years previously my partner and I found my name chalked high on the cliff face in what looked like my own hand-writing. Here, by the ruined hermitage, there are 3 wonderful labyrinths, possibly thousands of years old, carved into the rock under the ledges. Across the close by wooden bridge, over the vibrant little River Trevillet, that spilled from St. Nectan's Glen, and one suddenly feels about as remote from the world as any authentic labyrinth would have you be.

After a brief whip around Boscastle, the little harbour town that was almost washcd away in 2004, and home to the witchcraft museum, we headed for home.

It wasn't long after we had driven past Tintagel that all of a sudden Dave clapped his hands, slapped his cheeks and exclaimed, *"Of course! Of course! Bloody 'ell! I've just remembered!"*

"What? what?"

"You know that guy you were talking to yesterday – Dennis? The one who was chased by a UFO near Tintagel! And he met those two guys. . . Well, IT WAS OUTSIDE THAT HOTEL!!"

When I got back home I looked up the Castle Hotel Tintagel on the internet: www.camelotcastle.com

Here are some of the comments from hotel guests – some of whom are obviously from another dimension. Guess which ones:

"A truly magnificent place"

"We had a magical stay"
"Thanks very warmly"

"by far the creepiest experience I have ever encountered."

"it was faithfully supported by 3 legs and a stack of books on Scientology."
"a shower was a cubicle plonked in the middle of the bedroom"

Discovered the L Ron Hubbard machines in the downstairs lounge area. If you are a scientologist - the perfect retreat. You can be regressed apparently. The artwork was a little strange. Ted Stourton 'Outsells Picasso' apparently (or he did when I stayed there!). I think the owners have great belief in themselves.

"The "World's Greatest Living Artist" makes powerful statements by putting irridescent butterfly stickers in the corners of his paintings, which are mostly fat brush strokes of color. There were Scientology books on in the lobby book rack, and we began to get the feeling that we had landed in a Scientology recruiting station. The gourmet dinner was excellent, and exceeding expensive (not included in the stay). We noticed John Mappin entertaining a table full of suckers and wondered if they were being converted. We were not invited to see the "Light Box" (thank God!)."

Travel reviews, I have no doubt at all, are frequently crammed with plants from friends and rivals alike but when I first read the reviews on the hotel there were heaps of comments from people who said things like: *We think the previous glowing reviews are pants and were written by the owners or their friends.* [51]

---

[51] www.cornwalls.co.uk/accommodation_review-1092.htm
http://ca.answers.yahoo.com/answers2/frontend.php/question?qid=20070922065358AAnqHbh

I found this link on Google. It's a two-part article where the second part (that the below comments belong to) has gone walkabout. Funny that! Abracadabra . . . make it come back!

If anyone is any doubt that Tripadvisor is open to abuse then look up the reviews of Camelot Castle in Tintagel. The difference between the genuine reviews and those clearly authored by the owner (he name checks himself in almost everyone) is staggering. He's even started chiding himself for the small bathrooms!!! [52]

The castle scribes have been working overtime methinks.
So that's what the rooms in the cellar are for.
It all seems so very strange . . . and right somehow:

In case the reader is unaware, Scientology is no stranger to aliens and teaches that the human soul is a ? they call a thetan (pronounced like 'Satan' but with a lisp - not that Satan's got one. At least I haven't heard that he has).

http://en.wikipedia.org/wiki/Thetan
http://en.wikipedia.org/wiki/Xenu

Aliens, Extraterrestrials, and Xenu
www.scientology-lies.com/faq/teachings/aliens.html

The Un- Funny Truth http://theunfunnytruth.ytmnd.com

High light

One afternoon my friends Penny and Mary and I met at Mary's house for a meditation. We sat down in a circle around a little low table in Mary's snug meditation room put on some soft music and lit a candle which was placed in the middle of the table. After a while I opened my eyes to see the candle flame leave the candle and float at least 3 feet above it. I glanced around at Penny who was staring wide-eyed at the sight but Mary was still meditating and missed it.

On another occasion, I think it was only Mary and I this time, a large candle melted into a stunningly life-like sculpture of a hooded monk.

---

[52] www.travelcentre.com.au/Hotel%20review%20websites%20a%20%20five-star%20scam2.htm

My World

I took my Tarot cards out to the table under the back veranda it was one of those still, baking hot mornings in Perth, too hot to do anything. I was sheltered here though, in the corner under the UV shaded roof. I was experimenting with Tarot lays, just following whatever came. After shuffling them I laid down a line of cards and placed the remaining deck face down on the table to my left. At once the top card of the deck rose in the air floated across me and landed face up in perfect alignment with the other cards. It was the card called 'The World'.

Five
COMPANIONS & WATCHERS

My primary concern, when 'contact' ramped up in April '96, was for my girlfriend and she in turn, obviously, was worried for her two children more than for herself. There was no one we could talk to and anyway, if there was, what could they do?

At the core of me I understood that the inevitable consequence of centuries of rationalism, whether or not it was by design (I tend to think it has been) was bound to breed a docile, imperceptive and dependent human herd entirely detached on every level from the profusion of life in the universe. So, where, especially in a small suburb of Perth, the most isolated city in the world was I going to find anyone who was not so afflicted?

'The System' does not encourage freethinkers it actively discourages them through its credentialed examinations; the emphasis it puts on intellectualism even, perhaps especially, for vocations that are crucial to human health and well-being. Assuredly, and conveniently for the agenda (I'm so amazed), this has encouraged emotional retardation and dissuaded more sensibly rounded aspirants. So doctors are out . . . though I did try a couple, and should have listened to myself.

I've found in life that if I want advice about somewhere or something the very best thing to do is to ask someone who has actually been there or done it before. It isn't always possible and it is rare that two situations are absolutely the same but I'd still rather the pilot had actually flown the plane before.

Well, at the time, all I had to go on was my own recollections of previous encounters and I was still here, even though at the point of going to sleep I never know whether I'll still be here in the morning. That's the problem. In some ways I know the experience too well and that wasn't what my beautiful partner would want to hear. In my heart though I knew she and her children were ok. I know that my contacts are a contract and part of this contract is that none of my friends and loved ones are injured (by them) in any way. They are necessary companions and watchers in my journey just like I am in theirs; soul lessons are a part of every communication we have with everyone that our energetic array meets.

It is only possible to communicate with something else if a channel is compatible and the communicants can perceive and comprehend each other. Any intervention with these beings could only be achieved by someone *wired* to converse on the level of reality they inhabit and the only person I knew well enough then, in Australia, who had been to their world and talked to them, was me.

I spoke to my *otherworld* visitors and guardians about my partner and I was told that the fear she had would subside. I was also shown some previous lives we had shared together and from this I gathered that her role in all this was significant and that once her earthly manifestation merged with her spirit over this then all would be well. I pictured a person standing under a waterfall with the water pouring onto their head. The water represented eternal knowledge and wisdom and the meaning of the picture was obvious - understand (and be). There was clearly a purpose to this.

For now though, my partner needed some assurance from somebody neutral to the situation and crucially, who wasn't going to judge or ridicule her.

When ordained reality insists from every quarter that there is nothing outside the box but now and again a pesky Jack jumps out and says, 'Yes there is!' they're not best pleased. They rally their tin soldiers, *Plods* and *Noddies*: 'Look at our (or our guru's) university educations, combed hair and fat salaries; and what about our (their) big cars, bank accounts and houses, status and influential friends . . . and we have privileged access to NASA you know . . . '

That's another thing about 'The System', it builds up the people who pander to it the most and then one day something happens to each one of them; then they admit that what they have is ill-gotten corrupt or unjust but they have too much to lose now. The 'Big S' can just as soon demolish them and it might do anyway, if it feels like it. But meanwhile:

"These reports are just nonsense; merely the ravings of mistaken people (you know they want to say loonies), unsophisticated, poorly educated people or (what they really intend to say) self-seeking liars!"

Yet, you, the person who is there, at the coalface of the truth mine, you know different and gradually you understand that not only is convention wrong about the nature of reality those who dictate these things know that they are wrong. Almost everything we are told to believe about the expression of all life is untrue.

Immediately we recognise that the dichotomy of the *real world* and the *illusion* where what we are brow-beaten by worldly authorities to believe is the proper one, real (and therefore pass our lives away following) is just a lesser dimension copy of the true experiential environment.

Harvard psychiatrist Professor John Mack understood this and he devoted his life to investigating realms that convention shies away from - otherworlds and their inhabitants and how they interact with our world - which inevitably meant that he would get involved with the 'Alien abduction' phenomenon. Dr. Mack became very well known for his research into these subjects. He was also, unusually for a scientific man, very compassionate. Even though he lived and worked in America I wrote to him right at the beginning of the events in April '96. There was nobody with anything like his experience to talk to in Australia and I was desperate to find some help for my girlfriend. Part of it, for me too, was just to have someone to talk to, someone intelligent, who understood, and knew about the subject. Dr Mack didn't let me down and although he didn't say much in his initial letter to me he acknowledged us, and more importantly the experience. It meant so much.

Dr. Mack was part of the establishment and it is a strong likelihood that he, and his research, was used by it for their own purposes.

I attended a conference in Glastonbury, at which he spoke, only weeks before he was killed by *a drunken driver* in London. Dr. Mack was out for a stroll and it seems that he may have momentarily forgotten that people drive on the left in the UK. It's one of those incidents that I'm sure Dr. Mack himself, could easily have seen as being within the capabilities of mind-control, possession whatever you want to call it and quite possibly both. There is no room for a compassionate man in the laboratories of the New World Order. [53]

---

[53] The website of the late Dr. John Mack: www.johnmack.com

P·E·E·R

PROGRAM FOR EXTRAORDINARY EXPERIENCE RESEARCH

September 6, 1996

Dear Ellis,

Just wanted to drop you a quick note to let you know I received
your letter.

The photographs you sent are very interesting. I have seen similar
photos taken by abductees. Whether or not your experiences are
indicative of an abduction, however, is another matter. I do not
have a clear understanding of what is generating your experiences
and therefore recommend that you find a neutral listener with
whom to speak. As I feel it is important not to be isolated with this
information I am going to ask Roberta Colasanti at PEER to see if
she can send you the name of a support person in Australia.

Best Wishes,

John E. Mack, M.D.

1493 Cambridge Street, Cambridge, MA 02139 617.497.2667 Fax 617.497.0122

Another person that I wrote to was the retired Yorkshire detective,
author, and UFO and abduction researcher, Tony Dodd, another lovely
man whose support helped beyond words in those early days. Tony
wrote what I think is one of the best books in the genre, Alien
Investigator.

I'd seen a video of Tony and in a remarkable piece of *coincidence* I was
given his book for a birthday present. The reason why I contacted Tony
initially was because in an account in the book he mentions how another
experiencer had been given the same message as I had, "Peace, no harm."[54]

---

[54] ALIEN INVESTIGATOR, Headline Books, 1999, ISBN 0747222851

Sometimes I ponder on the incredibly complex threads that had to be knitted together in order for Mary, my partner, and I to meet. It seems obvious that ACERN is part of an agenda for good far bigger than all of us and one that derives from, and was instigated by a non-human intelligence. Certainly, without diminishing Mary's tremendous never-say-die attitude, the way has been made smooth so often when you wouldn't have given her numerous projects *Buckley's*. The media, for instance, is crammed with resolute sceptics and ill-informed people who scorn anything that convention baulks at but once they've entered the energy of the ACERN office and experienced the *Madge-blitzkrieg* they don't

Mary Rodwell and me at St. Nectan's waterfall in Cornwall.

stand a chance. Many a *Damascus Moment* has occurred in the leafy foothills of Perth. Good on ya mate.

She was there too

As I mentioned earlier, my girlfriend has had her own experiences and it is obvious that even though they have been terrifying she has gained a much broader perspective on life and what is possible. In many ways great positives have come of them. Here, she writes down, in her own words, some of those incidents, and her feelings around them. I think she's done a great job. She prefers to remain anonymous.

Found it really hard to fall asleep last night (Tuesday, 16th April) worried about Ellis and the possibility of another visitation by those Aliens.

Would of finally fallen asleep at about 2.00am (17th April). Not long after - felt like about 1/2 an hour or so, when I heard a tiny voice in my head whisper to me saying "their here". I woke quite startled and just then the door made a loud thump. The window was not open to cause the door to make the loud noise so I was perplexed as to how the door made the noise. I was immediately afraid. I quickly closed my eyes and then opened them very slowly and thought I saw fine lines at the bottom of the bed - electric green in colour and immediately closed and opened them again to clear my eyes in case I was imagining what I saw. Unfortunately there was nothing there the second time.

The whole atmosphere of the room changed to almost electric. I started to get frightened about what I might see. My heart was thumping furiously to the point I thought it was going to come out of my body. I was terrified and turned on my side facing Ellis. Ellis at this time was facing the wall. I started to feel really hot around me and had a sense of feeling that I was being watched too. Then a calm sensation overcame me and I started to relax but still lay wide awake watching.

I watched Ellis closely, as he tossed and turned occasionally gently rubbing his face with his left hand. He would then turn on to his stomach for a few minutes and then back on his back with one arm pinned above his head and one arm rested on his stomach. His breathing was heavy and fast and then heavy but slow. He would occasionally groan but not for long. His positions changes within the space of minutes. This went on for what seemed a lifetime but in real terms I guess would of been about 5-6 minutes. Then Ellis' breathing changed again and what seemed like he had stopped breathing. I listened closely and he was back to breathing very quietly as he normally would. There was then a sense of calmness in the air and I started to feel relaxed. I did not return to sleep – Ellis woke more. a couple of times to go to the toilet – the first time he said the light was on in the lounge room. He had remembered turning it off the previous night.

THIS IS... WHAT THE LINES LOOKED LIKE.

Thursday 25th April 1996.
shoved Head night of Thurs/Fri 25/26th
During the night (24th) Ellis & I went to bed
around 11.30 pm, perhaps slightly later. Ellis
fell asleep almost instantly and I lay awake
for some time before dozing. I noticed it was
very dark and although Ellis lay next to me
I could only just see the silhouette of his
face in the darkness.

I had fallen asleep after a short time of
noticing things around me (looking around from)
from the street came through the blinds
and reflected about 1 ft above Ellis' head
(on the bed head). Other than that it was
quite dark.

I woke through restlessness sometime
later, I figure it was well after midnight. I was facing Ellis and he was
laying on his back with his face slightly
tilted towards me. His face appeared strange.
He looked the same r however there seemed
a light now appeared on his face. Around
the nose and on part of his mouth. I
was a bit perplexed as previously I could

barely see his face. The light fascinated me + I waved my hand over it and I did not seem to have it over my hand. I wanted to be blocking it out. It just shone on his face. I then also noticed the white on the pattern of the pillowcase / doona cover also was illuminated, around the side of Ellis' cheek on the pillow case) and on the cover near his hand, (his hand was under the cover). The street light still appeared about a foot over the top of Ellis' head.

comment on how his nose and part of his cheek felt like he'd been sunburned. His face appeared only slightly red but nothing really noticeable. I then told him what I saw.

29 June 1997 Went to bed at approximately 12.30am - couldn't sleep. Mind was preoccupied with Ellis returning to Perth Thursday.

Sometime later (unsure of the time) the atmosphere of the room changed. The sounds of the traffic and night sounds could no longer be heard. There was a strange noise which could best be described as "buzzing" (only sound at this stage and seemed to be in my head). I also felt a shortage of breath. My eyes immediately felt very heavy and I could barely keep them open. I struggled with this for a couple of seconds but was pointless as the energy was too strong. My arms, legs and body at this precise moment were like "lead". I tried to move my arms and struggled once again, this time to move my body into a more comfortable position - but could not. (I was facing the windows of our bedroom - half on my back and half on an angle).

Finally giving in, my body started to tingle from the feet up. A surge of "energy" is the only way I can describe it, entered my body and drew me towards the very edge of the bed, almost to the point I was concerned I would end up with a thud on the floor, but somehow I didn't. I felt both my arms being held (by an increased pressure of energy not hands). My body still maintaining the same position was turned around and drawn towards the end of the bed and back up again. This happened twice (completing 2 full circles of the bed) as if to be hypnotised. I then went blank. The next thing I remember, I was in a large empty room being made to follow two women. Both had nurse-like uniforms (one had short brown hair and fairly stocky (she wore a light green uniform) and the other was slightly built and had short mousy blond hair (she wore a white uniform). I was not able to see their faces and no words were spoken however I just "knew" as if telepathically I was to go with them. We entered a lift and once the doors closed I passed out once again. I regained my consciousness in another smaller room and was woken by the sound of soft music (it was a ballad type song sung by a male and female (doing a duet)). I am unable to remember the song, however, I feel sure if I hear it again I will remember it. This was my last recollection until I woke up rather suddenly back in my bed in exactly the same position bodywise, however my arms were straight down by my side.

At this stage I must say, I did not feel convinced that it was all over. A little nervous about what might happen next, I turned on the light to check the time and it was 2.30am.

After turning off the light, the noises of the night soon started to dissipate once again. However, I was determined this time to stay in full control. Suddenly the dog (who was sleeping in my daughter's room at the end of the hall) started to bark frantically. The door to my daughter's room was open which meant that the dog could see our bedroom door from where he was. I heard my daughter tell him to be quiet. I then realised that the atmosphere of the room had within an instant returned to "normal" and I proceeded to turn on the light. I calmed the dog down and patted him, he was at my door by this stage, took my little girl to the toilet, returned her and the dog to their respective beds and went back to bed myself.

As soon as I settled down, as if within minutes the atmosphere instantly changed, obliterating all the sounds from outside and I found myself once again paralysed. After this I do not remember what happened, however, I woke at 7.05am feeling extremely tired, as if I had not been to bed at all that night. Later that morning, I started to bleed (as if I had a period). This I felt was not possible as I had had one almost 2 weeks before. My head also hurt particularly over the right eye and I felt extremely flushed and with an adrenalin rush which continued for most of the day.

The following account was written by my partner about an experience she had in Perth, Australia in 1997 while I was in the UK.

Couldn't sleep last night – 5 July 1998 (2.45am).

Felt a cold and tingly sensation all over me, as I closed my eyes. Felt the distinct presence of someone near me in bed. While my eyes were closed, my body seemed to move to the right side of the bed and I felt as though I was going to fall of the edge. At the same time I seemed to see images as if they were on a black and white TV screen. I was firstly 'welcomed' by what appeared to be an 'alien'. His (I say 'his' because it was a soft but deep male voice) and his words were exactly "We welcome you". His mouth did not move but I 'knew' what he was saying – telepathically I guess.

Then I felt as if I was flying – over tops of buildings, but still in black and while TV images. I went over old buildings, the San Francisco Bridge, Manhattan and suddenly I was witnessing bombs falling through a blackened sky. It was an eerie and sad feeling – the feeling of a lot of death and destruction. I was scared a little by these images and felt my breathing get heavier.

Then I felt the overwhelming need to see who was next to me as I lay in bed. I felt paralysed though and struggled to open my eyes and move my head to the left of me (which I eventually did). I saw an 'alien type' figure lying next to me on its back on top of the covers. It was a short gaze and as soon as 'it' realised that I was watching, the thin figure stood up and moved to the half open bedroom door. The door opened fully and oddly the light went on in the hallway. The figure walked into the hallway without any emotion or glance at me. The door then closed slowly and the light went out. That was all I remembered.

Continued:

When I woke in the morning, seeing the door was still closed – I 'knew'
that something had happened in the night, because when I went to bed
the door was open. A habit of mine I guess. When my daughters are
away from home, my bedroom door always stays open. When they are
home I always closed it before getting into bed.

For the first time I was not afraid at my experience. But what does it all
mean? What was I being shown and why? All the images I had seen
were still clear to me. Had I not opened my eyes to see what or who was
next to me what else would I have been shown? Will they

Mary's skill and experience as a counsellor helped my partner on the
way to eventually dealing with these radical changes to her life and from
these strange events that happened in a small suburban house in Perth,
Western Australia an organisation grew that was to assist thousands.

Mary Rodwell joined with another counsellor called Elizabeth
Robinson to form the Australian Close Encounters Resource Network
(ACERN); not long afterwards Elizabeth resigned and Mary drew on her
martial sign, Aries, determined to do battle with the world on behalf of
the countless experiencers who were drawn to her. She's a remarkable
lady, and a great friend.

Click

I was outside a block of apartments in the centre of Oxford when a
small car veered across the road and pulled up beside me. The driver, a
man in his early 30s, called out asking me if I knew where the Randolph
Hotel was. I did and so I gave him directions, which he repeated. As I
leant down I heard a click and looked over to see his female passenger
brandishing a camera at which they sped off. A similar thing happened a
few days later, on the 16th November 2006. I was chatting to my
neighbour when a car drove slowly past while the driver twice held a
mobile phone out of his window, and across his bonnet, pointed in our
direction. "Who's that?" I asked my companion. "I don't know, never seen
him or the car before," he replied.

We know where you live

Several years ago I was asked to appear on Perth's Channel 7 to talk about my 'abduction' experiences. Although I was suffering quite badly with asthma at the time the interview went quite well.

Afterwards when chatting with the TV crew I suggested to them that an interesting programme for them to do would be to televise a hypnosis session with a man who was being hounded by police and media who was supposedly the chief suspect in the so-called 'Claremont Serial Killer' crimes - providing that is that the man was willing. Clearly there was no evidence against this man. A hypnotist I knew had been very involved in obtaining the release of another man who had been wrongly convicted of murder. The TV people were very enthused at this and began to set it up. The hypnotist was more than willing to help but was later made aware in no uncertain terms that some police officers were not happy about it.

That night, after my interview was aired, the phone rang:

"Could I speak to Ellis Taylor?" It was a man's voice, measured and serious and I didn't recognise it.

"Speaking..."

"Oh, hello. We're from Channel 9 and we've just finished one job; we are only up the road from you and wondered if we could call round quickly for a brief interview?"

Something about this felt very odd. Questions ran through my head . . . like how do they know my telephone number? And how do they know where I live? It too seemed very unprofessional. They didn't come round and a call to Channel 9 the next day confirmed that the caller was nothing to do with them.

Hell-o...up here

Soon after Dr. David Kelly's body was discovered I wrote up two articles on the manifold occult aspects of the incident on my website. During my research I was in communication with a lady called Rowena Thursby (who later started a blog). [55]

---

[55] Dr. David Kelly: www.ellisctaylor.com/harrowdown.html
http://dr-david-kelly.blogspot.com

At one point while I sat at the computer, writing the article and exchanging emails with Rowena, a military helicopter sat above my house then flew in a tight circle before moving off when I mentioned it on email. Rowena has been like a dog with a bone with the Kelly tragedy and is very involved with doctors and forensic professionals who have strong doubts about the official theory; they are called the Kelly investigation Group.

I have had military helicopters over houses that I'm living, or staying at, so many times that I've lost count now. There was one over the house for an age last night (7th November 2008); it was so loud it drowned the TV out. I put up with it for 10 minutes then went outside to look for it. The helicopter was very high and directly over the house. I ran to get my camera and as soon as the flash went off it moved away rapidly to the North West.

There have been several occasions, out in the countryside, when I have been hovered over, even swooped on, by military helicopters, but I'm not the only one this happens to. I once met some people who had spent the eve of the Summer solstice on top of Silbury Hill, near Avebury in Wiltshire, who had been terrified by a military helicopter hovering just a few feet above their heads! Military intimidation using helicopters is regularly reported by crop circle enthusiasts. I've seen them over crop circles myself - and photographed them.

In October 2000 Paul, Ann, Daniel and Jason Andrews came to Perth, in Western Australia, where I was living at the time. We met up on several occasions and a couple of days before they were to return to England they came round to our house for a barbeque. I invited my family and some friends around too, during the evening a helicopter hovered over our house for several minutes - much to the excitement of some of the children attending, and terror to others.

Infernal

I never did find out who it was but this wasn't an isolated case. I've mentioned other examples of intimidation and harassment already but on the magical date of 28th February (2003) - after I'd predicted on my website something infernally serious for that date - a huge fire started mysteriously close to my home. It swept across the field heading directly for our street when suddenly (and inexplicably according to members of the fire crew) it changed direction and roared away South to the river. I mentioned this on my website:

"The night of Friday 28th February, between the hours of 7pm and 8pm a fire ignited at the eastern end of a field that borders my house. The fire swept west with the strong wind, to the river and then jumped the river to consume a vineyard. The river is just beyond the trees, in the picture (below). Had the wind direction changed, or been blowing in a slightly more northerly direction, my house and scores of others would now be history. And the possibility of people losing their lives doesn't bear thinking about. A big thank you too to the dozens of fire fighters who attended. Fantastic work guys!

This picture is taken from near my house, about 250-300 metres away from the fire. Someone's dog was not so fortunate. This morning a fireman found the beagle-like dog dead in a clearing.

This is yet another example of what I have been alerting everyone to over the last few days. And possibly the reason the fire struck with such perfect timing (It is an 8 day - also see below.) 8 is a fire number. A dog is an 8 animal. Vineyard is an 8. Just a few degrees difference in the wind direction and you might not have been reading this. It is perfectly possible that this fire was majickally summoned against me. Fortunately someone up there was taking care of us. You might want to draw your own conclusions.

An example of what could be for those who challenge the system, educate and inform humanity to the horrors that lurk where they don't bother looking? And all on top of blacked-out cars loitering outside the front of our house, low-flying buzzing helicopters over our house and when I'm walking in the countryside, silent phone calls, threatening phone calls, tapped phone lines, computer hacking and viruses etc etc.." [56]

I was a bit upset, as you can see.

Culbone Church

As I glanced up from where I laid in the sun soaked grass below a huge sarsen in the northern circle of the Avebury complex a tall, svelte, middle-aged woman in a flowing dress approached me. She sat for a while and then she asked me for healing. She had a troubled soul, was certainly psychic and I sensed that she had a deep fear within her about which she could not, and as it turned out, would not talk. She asked me where I was travelling to . . . A question I knew encompassed several

---

[56] www.ellisctaylor.com/eclipse.html

meanings but I held to the obvious one and told her how I was making my way down to the southwest. She suggested that I visit 'the smallest church in the kingdom' at a place called Culbone on the north Devon/Somerset coast. I felt a chill but she assured me that it was a beautiful spot in heavenly scenery. I'd never heard of Culbone before but I'll never forget it. This was in the summer of 1996.

We bade farewell and I made for the Avebury Henge Shop. Half an hour or so later I emerged to see the lady walking towards me again. She asked if I could take her to Glastonbury where she lived. As I was heading for Glastonbury myself for an appointment with UFO Reality magazine the next day I agreed. It was dark when we reached her home so I said goodbye and drove up the hill to sleep in my car near the Tor. As I neared the top of the road a bright white light zoomed silently from left to right across dark blue sky parallel to the horizon in front of me. (This object was also witnessed by someone else who had reported it to 'UFO Reality' prior to our meeting.) As I parked up I noticed that the woman had left a scarf on the passenger's seat. I decided that I'd return it in the morning, which I did.

At first light I climbed to the top of Glastonbury Tor, the landscape so breathtaking in the mists of dawn, and then drove back into the town centre. After an enjoyable time at UFO Reality magazine's offices I delivered the scarf and set out to investigate Glastonbury Abbey and the town centre. It was a beautiful day and my next stop would be Somerset and Culbone church.

I arrived at the track to Culbone around 4.45p.m. and parked near a gate. The track went uphill to a farm and downhill to the church. I grabbed my camera and holdall and sauntered down the steep-ish incline and into the moss-laden and sombre tree lined avenue. On either side were remnants of old stone walls and ramparts. The road was much longer than I thought and as I tramped along the trees conveyed a very un-tree-like energy, if not menace. It really felt like they were watching me. The sun rarely, if ever, ventured into this musty tree-cave that was funnelling me into somewhere I was beginning to feel very uneasy about. I recalled my initial reaction, a chill, to the woman's suggestion to visit this place while we lolled in the warm mid-summer sunshine of Avebury. It seemed so long ago. I did consider going back and forgetting about Culbone church. I hadn't heard or seen any birds or animals let alone people, and that occurred to me to be odd. Even the name was beginning to sound ominous . . . Cull and bone, but I'd come this far. [57]

After a while I came to a sharp right-hand bend and in a few more paces I could see stone houses, just one or two...and sunlight...of a sort. I passed the first building (a mill at one time I pondered) and wound around to the little church topped by a witch's hat steeple and sporting a tall cross in the yard at its fore. I explored the church building's exterior and then tried the door. It was open and I ventured in. There was no one else about; I hadn't seen a soul since I drove from the main road. A pleasant enough building to look at, quite plain but to be honest I don't  remember much about it. As soon as I entered the empty church this almost whispered, but clear voice, right at my side, cracked urgently through the silence, "GET OUT...NOW!!!". It wasn't an order, it wasn't threatening, and the tone was unmistakeably earnest, benign and protective. Well, I didn't need telling twice...I threw open the door to be met with a glowering twilight. It was too early! I raced out the churchyard through the looming branches reaching out to my stumbling form and along the terrifying two miles of this sinister passage. All the while the voice accompanied me, encouraging me on, "You are safe... keep going... don't look back...you are always protected!' And I did feel strangely secure. And I got there, the other side of the woods...and it was daylight, 6.35p.m.!

A couple of years later, on another trip to The Isles from Australia, I returned to Culbone church. I went much earlier in the day this time. Again I didn't see anyone and yet again there was a sinister air pervading the place, but perhaps it was less so this time. I saw a blackbird, and a sparrow I think it was, but that was all. The mill house (?) looked occupied, the church was locked and everything was I suppose quite normal. A week later I called on a friend. He showed me a photograph of a little church on the Somerset coast. Right across the photograph an eerie black band had manifested on the print. Apparently the photograph

---

[57] Culbone is apparently derived from 'Kil Beun', Church of St Beuno - Not recommended for people called 'Beun'.

was sent to my friend by retired policeman and UFO researcher John Hanson... and you've guessed it, it was a photograph of Culbone church.

I looked up Culbone on Google and came across an enlightening excerpt from a book on Culbone written by Joan Cooper. Although legend says that Christ came here in AD25 it seems Culbone has been a place of dread for a very long time - dark sorcerers, wretched lepers, the insane, heretics, every manner of outcast stricken, deemed and chosen.[58]

Fairy Dell

Artists John Pickering and Katie Hall live in the Lake District. Their home is an atmospheric old Edwardian house set in grounds overflowing with flowers, woods and water. In this literally enchanted setting they have captured the most remarkable light phenomena which they describe and show in their fascinating book, 'Beyond Photography ~ Encounters with orbs, angels and mysterious light-forms.'[59]

John and Katie are lovely people and we have become friends. In October 2006 I went to stay with them for a few days. In the evenings we ventured out, cameras in hand, in the hope of capturing some of the ephemeral inhabitants of the *Fairy Dell* - as Katie likes to call their little wood. Every night, in some photos, we captured orbs but one night I left Katie and John in the dell and walked down their drive. A little way along I was suddenly aware that I was being followed. I looked behind but could see nothing yet I still had the sense that something was there. It was a rather eerie feeling and I began to think that I was being stalked. By now it was extremely dark and I looked behind me a couple of times but still could not see anything. All of a sudden I heard and felt something flash past me to my right, the leaves on the bushes flickered and I clicked the camera shutter. I stopped and pressed the button on the back of the camera to see if I had caught whatever it was.

[58] 'Culbone a Spiritual History': www.minehead-online.co.uk/culbone.htm
[59] *Beyond Photography*, John Pickering and Katie Hall, O Books, www.lights2beyond.com

Some people see the figure of a bird, perhaps an owl, flying towards the camera; the head of some creature in the top right - very dinosaur-like. The tree behind seems to be having trouble deciding whether to be here or somewhere else. Actually the dinosaur-like head features in another photograph taken by John and Katie I think, on a previous occasion. It belongs to a creature that looks to me as if it hunting another.

I hurried back up the drive to where Katie and John were and before I could say anything John, with a stunned expression on his face, said look at this. Placing his camera in my hands I looked at the back screen to see Katie standing right where she was now and looking at her camera screen; and looking like its right cheek is pressed to Katie's forehead a huge grey wolf, with a cat sitting on a tree branch above, both made of the same ephemeral mist as the *creatures* I'd just filmed. Incredible stuff!

On a later visit to the Lake District I visited John and Katie's home with Mike Oram and Fran again capturing orbs on some photographs. When we were about to go Mike and Fran had just crossed over to the other side of the stream. As I aimed my camera to take a photo I heard a rustle at my feet looked down to see a plump, round-cheeked little face which stared up at me and then dived quickly back into the undergrowth. I was open-mouthed but speechless at first but then I rushed over the little bridge to Mike and Fran and told them what I'd just seen: "I've just seen a gnome or something! It was in the grass by that tree . . . and it was looking up at me and it just went . . . " I excitedly recounted.

"Fran was just saying that she heard something in the grass there just then," says Mike in his laid-back, unruffled way.

"I did. We were wondering what it was," Fran said. "Something about it seemed odd."

When I tuned into the energy of the place I sensed that this house belonged to people who practiced magic and had some connection to Aleister Crowley. Their workings caused a rip in space and time creating an entrance (and exit) for all sorts of beings. I saw the 'gnome' in what seems to be the most active spot in the wood; it is also where the wolf was photographed. [60]

---

[60] www.popsubculture.com/pop/bio_project/aleister_crowley.html

My friend Wally

At the beginning of the 80s I lived on a farm. One lunchtime I was told that a baby owl had fallen out of its nest which was in one of the barns. I rushed over to where I was told I'd find it and sure enough there it was an ugly little bugger with a bundle of grey feathers. I fetched a ladder and gently put the little fella back inside the dark tubular metal beam as far as I could. I waited a while and nothing happened so I went back to finish my meal. About 10 minutes later I returned to the barn and the little owl chick was again laying in the straw below the nest. Twice more I returned it to its nest but each time out it came again.

Poor little thing, I knew by then that if I didn't look after it then it would not survive. In another barn there was an old cupboard. I stuffed a cardboard box with straw put a small shallow dish of water next to it and pinched a bit of the cats' food then I phoned a few wildlife parks and asked if they could take in the little bird - but there was no room at the inns at that time of year. I knew that it was a 'Little Owl' because we had seen its parents flying about the barn and I asked the sanctuaries for advice on how to care for it.

Wally grew up to be one of the best companions I've ever had. He feared nothing cats would scarper like the wind if he was around. Many a time - and he only had to do it once - cats had the tables turned on them. I took him to work with me whenever I could and he'd amuse himself chasing bugs and ducking the other birds that dive-bombed him all day long - it seemed that he had an instinctive indifference to their threats and he took little notice of them. When it was time to go I'd give a little whistle and over he'd come straight away, sit on my arm, or my shoulder, and I'd put him in the car. On the way to and from work he'd perch on the back of the front passenger seat watching everything. We used to get some strange looks.

One beautiful blue-sky Sunday I was busy gardening, Wally was sitting on the shed roof dodging martins when I was called in for dinner. That was the last time I saw Wally.

Curious creatures

On 5th October 2004 I was out in the back garden at home when I looked up at the sky and saw a white ball of light in the east. I took 3 photographs in rapid succession, or as fast as my digital camera can go anyway. I wasn't aware of anything else being around at all but when I

looked at the pictures on the computer the following photos show what was looking back at me! To me it looks like a small herd of curious *otherworld* creatures. I might not have been aware of them but, by their demeanour they were interested in what I was up to. Do they remind you of how horses and cows are fascinated by the things we humans do?

The photographs are in order. They all show the white ball of light in the middle of the frame - which may have been a shuttle or something.

In Photo 1 an orange tube or, ribbon-like thing has appeared.
In Photo 2 this has disappeared but in the bottom right there is a tiny orange glow.
In Photo 3 there they are.

Wish I'd known. How excellent is that!

* If you would like to have a colour copy of photo 3 then please visit my website where I use it as a background. www.ellisctaylor.com

I'm a point and press man when it comes to photography, I didn't use any special settings - just the simple mode.

Return to Long Sutton

Now it might seem that I am a glutton for punishment, after what happened in September '06 but I returned for a weekend visit to the Andrews in the November. Paul, Ann and Jason are really good friends

A view from Jason's former bedroom window - notice the abundant diamond-shaped orbs.

and I enjoy my visits. I've never experienced anything traumatic at their house before. I've heard, seen and felt some unusual things, UFOs, beings and weird mists and vortices etc. I've woken up with marks on my body there too and there have been times when I have a feeling that something has occurred but I can never remember what. I usually sleep wonderfully well at their house. Besides visiting my friends the reason I returned was that I wanted to confirm the events of my last visit.

A few days prior to my leaving for Long Sutton this time I had an email from Fran, who you might recall was also staying at the Andrews' house that weekend. She wrote to let me know her recollections of the circumstances of my arrival on the previous visit. It confuses me even more. Where Ann, Paul and I remember Ann opening the door to me when I turned up Fran says that she thought she did. Fran writes:

1. I thought I opened the door to you! I definitely opened it to someone and it wasn't Jason and co cos I was sitting on the settee when they arrived. The only other person who arrived was you.

2. I am confused as to whether it was just getting dusk or was actually dark. I feel that when I opened the door it was still lightish but my memory of us all in the conservatory is that it was quite dark - and we were really only in there, at the most, 10 - 15 minutes I'd guess, after you arrived. Also, I had only just gone into the conservatory and don't think I was sitting down but was still in the doorway by the end of the sofa when Paola saw you. I feel that when I was in the conservatory it was starting to rain cos I heard it on the conservatory roof but when I opened the door you were not wet and I don't remember it raining outside.

3. Ann came out of the kitchen, greeted you and we all went into the conservatory. Once in the conservatory you sat at the little table. Ann asked if you'd like a cup of tea and went off to make it. I asked you if you were OK as I felt you weren't and you said you felt a bit 'weird' and could you have something to eat. (That was when I noticed your hands were shaking). I asked if you had eaten that day and then I went into the kitchen to speak to Ann and said, "I think he could probably do with something to eat." I thought I then came back and Ann followed me and asked if a cheese sandwich would be OK.

It is almost as if there were 'two' arrivals! Sure there can't have been. (?!)

On Friday, 24th November I set off for Long Sutton at the same time as the previous visit and arrived at about 4pm. On the way I wanted to stop at the service station so that I could see if things were any different (or the same). For some reason I did not see it. Whether it was hidden by lorries I don't know. On my way back though I think I did spot it. I couldn't miss the huge signs announcing 'MacDonald's'. How odd that I didn't remember what the fast-food outlet was!? As well, the restaurant was down below the road. I remembered having to drive up a hill and then down onto the carriageway when I left. (It may be that that is the case but I couldn't see the full site from my vantage point this time.)

Now, before I go on I want to tell you about something else that happened to me. It was just after 7pm, about 7.10, on Thursday 23rd November (the day before I was to leave for Long Sutton again). I was typing on my computer when suddenly my head began to spin; I could not focus my eyes and I felt violently sick. At the same time, it is hard for me to describe this, but it was like all that was left of me was my essence. I crawled over to the side of the bed leaning against it, my mind reeling, my eyes closed, and I felt this intense cold. Everything was silent. I called out. Still feeling entirely drained I attempted to resume my writing but I was shaking and exhausted. Switching the computer off I decided to rest. The next morning I still felt unwell and considered cancelling my trip but decided that I would go.

For part of my journey I found myself taking a route that I had never used before and it was during this section that my health returned. Nothing out of the ordinary happened over the weekend but I was able to find out a little more concerning my mysterious arrival on the previous occasion.

Ann and Paul are sure that I arrived when it was dark and that it was not raining when Ann opened the door to me. There was one other person I intended to ask, which I hoped would settle the matter once and for all; and that was Jason. When I turned up this time Jason and Jacqui were busy working on their car in the

Jason speaking at the PROBE Conference - with a *friend* and appearing to be *shape shifting* (note the other people in the photo are not blurred at all.

garage. Ann and Paul made me a cuppa and while we were sitting chatting Jason and Jacqui came in. A bit later in the conversation I turned to Jason and said, "While I think about it Jace . . . "

"Six!" he said, before I could go any further.

"Six what?" I asked (knowing full well that he had read my mind – which he does with anyone with ease). "How do you know what the question is?" Ann and I asked in chorus.

"Well finish the question and the answer is 6," Jason smiled.

"What time did you arrive on that Friday mate?" I enquired.
"Six, I told you," he grinned.
"No, it wasn't, that was when we phoned after picking Sacha up," said Jacqui. "Don't you remember? . . . So it must have been about 6.30-ish when we got here."

To tell you the truth, I'm more confused than ever by this time. Anyway I left it.

Later that evening I was telling them all about what had happened to me the previous evening. I had only got to the bit where my eyes could not focus when Jay said, *"EMP"* (electro-magnetic pulse) weapon. *"The same thing happened to me twice when I was in Italy, in the hotel. It is horrible. Did your aura disappear? Mine did; and it took a long time before I felt well again."*

That, I would say, is precisely what happened to me, my aura was dissolved, taken, whatever. I tried to describe it by saying that all that was left was my essence. But I have my aura back now.

I also showed Jason the red patch under my throat – which had returned to dark red again after the Thursday evening episode. "That's radiation!" he said.

When I have returned from my *otherworld* encounters I almost always have a kind of sunburn; it's sore, and usually very red. Lots of times I have an upset stomach too. After the episode with the dogs you will

recall that I told you how my hair was falling out and my beard stopped growing for days. A frequent memory of several occasions has me in a very bright room with figures in what look very like the white decontamination suits you see.

Two days after my return from Long Sutton I discovered that the person who Dean Warwick had claimed to know from Scotland had experienced something very similar on the previous day to me. This person was left partially and temporarily paralysed. I am pleased to report that they too are ok now.

"They think we know something Ell," they ventured. "What is it?"

Six
BECAUSE THEY ARE HERE MATE

Contrary to what everyone is led to believe very, very few people talk about the strange things they encounter in their lives; and why would they? We're informed that humans who come forward to recount their contact with otherworlds and beings are merely chasing glory or making up stories to make money. Well, let me tell you there is little or no money in this field and there is certainly no glory.

The best a person can expect from our current *Darkly* inspired and controlled world is a quick mention on a miserably moronic TV show presented by *Snide and Smirk* and then over to the ads.

I don't insist that people blindly believe what I tell them; in fact it would horrify me if they did, but in my world every soul has a dignity that requires respect. Why do so many media types, who are only animated talking sticks when all said and done, believe that it is their business to judge someone about something that they have no experience of? It isn't required. Their job is to present. It is not to try to sway audiences with their ignorance.

There must always be exceptions though and for me one was Mark Cagney and Sinead Desmond of Ireland's 'Ireland AM' on TV3. Mark Cagney is a talented professional man fair glowing with an easy respect and it was clear that Mr Cagney took the subject in his stride. Paola Harris and I were interviewed on the show by him  and Sinead Desmond. Ms Desmond, who was quite new to the show, I could tell was unsettled by the subject, but she dealt with her personal discomfort with a thorough professionalism. Big thanks; I wish there were more like you. [61]

---

[61] Ireland am: www.tv3.ie/programmes.php?action=irelandam

This was more than could be said for the rag drop-kick who murdered trees to write nearly a whole page on me without saying more than 'Hi' during the conference. Mind you she did slur something unintelligible to a group of us on the Saturday night when she fell out of a nightclub door to have a smoke, but that doesn't count, does it?

Although any appearances by people who are involved with the 'paranormal' are big audience draws TV shows don't pay their guests anywhere near adequate expenses - often the guest has lost a day's pay just to play Aunt Sally for some pathetic over-stuffed *thicko* who believes that they are the font of all wisdom and wit.

When these experiences invade your life *full on* they come like an earthquake with all the shake-up, chaos and division you would expect from that. Almost everything, especially mundane concerns, which you believed were so important, are revealed to be spurious distractions from what life is truly meant to be; but somehow you are expected to keep marching along to the robot beat with everyone else. That might be possible, depending upon how subdued your personality is, but eventually, even if it is on your deathbed, you will be obliged to acknowledge it. Despite all the brickbats that come with contact you realise that you have been privileged to catch an awesome glimpse of Creation.

What would you do?

For readers who have never had these kinds of experiences could I ask you to just take a moment to ponder on what you would do if they did begin to happen to you and/or someone you love? It could happen. Endless numbers of people, of all ages, and in every age, from every walk of life, have suddenly found themselves catapulted into this twilight world where they are forced to confront their cosy beliefs and buried fears. Any ideas on what you'd do?

Well, your first thoughts are that you are imagining things; perhaps you were dreaming, you know, maybe one of these *hypno-fads* that get trotted out. Worse still perhaps you are going nuts? Debunkers seem to think they are being original in their crass surety that experiencers never consider these things for themselves, but we all do . . . Ah, how tempting it might be, how comforting to think that a trip to a *trick-cyclist* or the pop of a doctor's pill will make it all go away . . . It doesn't and the tragedy is that experiencers throughout human history have been easy targets for the toxic remedies of every era's *gorms* and orthodox frigidity.

It doesn't help that most people still have a naive belief in the integrity of self-proclaimed spiritual authorities (science and religion) and government despite abundant evidence to the contrary. Consequently when someone like me comes along and rattles on about weird beings carting them off to other dimensions the average person doesn't think. They just respond according to the installed programming:

"Nuh mate! It can't be true. It can't be real otherwise our authorities and our experts would have told us. What about the papers mate? They've got people everywhere if there was something to it then they wouldn't take the piss would they?"

No mate, they wouldn't. You're right. I don't know what came over me. They wouldn't disparage, misrepresent and ridicule people who might be risking everything to report what they know to be true. Go back to sleep.

I'll tell you what I find unbelievable: that in this intimidating culture and atmosphere humans still believe that the truth is best served, encouraged and expressed.

So you've been visited in bizarre and frightening circumstances, you're not sleeping and there's never a moment in your house when the lights are not on. You can never be alone and every rustle of a leaf, tick of a clock, chirp of an insect and you're frying. You never shut the bedroom door but then you think that maybe it would be better to have it wide open, so you open it and get into bed then you think well, at least if it's shut they might not notice me. So you get up again and you shut the door and jump quickly back into bed then you think maybe I should turn the light off too - I'm too easy to see when the light's on and you flick off the switch but it's too dark . . . what was that? I saw something over there at the end of the bed, click! The light's back on but the door's shut. Oh no, the kids! I can't shut the door . . . and you're up and down like this all night, you half-sleep if you're lucky and the days and the nights meld into a twilight but the bills and other responsibilities are sharp, black and contrast. *They* might never come again. But you don't know that.

In time, though the memory of *them* is always there, you do manage to sleep, perhaps never again like you used to but you sleep. Then one night you go to bed and everything stops, all is silent, no cars, no insects no wind, no rain; silent streaks of vibrant colour, green mostly, flash everywhere and the brightest light you've ever seen erupts into the room. Suddenly there are figures moving around you in a strange discordant fashion and little garbled voices that you strain to hear but can't understand. You start to fizz and glow and you feel yourself lifting in the air. You look down at your partner (if you have one and they're still with you) and they are deeper in sleep than you've ever seen before and the bed covers are slowly wafting down back onto the bed. And you try to scream but nothing comes out and you're thinking, 'My God, what about the children!' and you call on everything you have to release you . . . and you're slowly floating back down onto the bed and you might see a light recede quickly into a wall or window or your door might slam BAM! And you jump, and there's a smell, it could be a sickly sweet hanging odour or it smells like acid like the last time . . . and you feel like you are on fire as if you've fallen asleep in the hot sun for hours and your skin is red and raw. What's those marks? Oh my God . . . I remember . . .

Can you imagine that?

All of these millions of souls striving to forget rather than process something that is so profound yet, in another way so elementary, contact with another form of life.

And on and on it goes, "Here mate, what you think you are experiencing must be *imagination*, a mental aberration of some kind!" And you say it to yourself. That contents your inner agent.

But then you start having more physical marks show up on your body, and you have unaccountable missing time and the incidents involve other people too. What happens then?

This is happening to countless numbers of people, people who are so scared of what the neighbours will say, what the doctors will say, what their family will say that they say nothing . . . to anybody. Many have children, and they are terrified for them because they too are showing signs of contact; they're talking about the  bright lights that wake them and *'the men'* who come into their room at night, waking with nose bleeds and inexplicable pains in their abdomen and it seems like there is nothing you can do. The best response they know they'll get is ridicule and the worst? Well, it doesn't bear thinking about; your kids are so special.

Believe me, as stupid as it is people still want to call you nuts. What was it Einstein said, *"Two things are infinite: the universe and human stupidity; and I'm not sure about the universe."* But it depends upon how you define stupidity because I don't think that humans are stupid - unless the word means entrained apathy and purposely indoctrinated ignorance. [62]

Life has taught me what it is like to live through bizarre incidents and to have strange beings intrude so often into my everyday world. When they do perhaps it is the frequencies of them that numbs me to their strangeness . . . But then, are these things really as strange as we are taught they are? What if they are not strange at all? We humans, with our excruciatingly limited range of perception, sense so little compared to other life forms on this planet that so readily respond to things that going on beyond our ken. Everything is a combination of energy and all energy communicates in some way. Life is everywhere and in everything - animal, mineral vegetable and more. It is we who 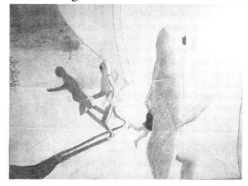 are the strangers here, we who would freeze were it not for fire yet shade our eyes from the sun, we who walk grimly aloof and ignorant, deaf, and blind through the tumultuous kaleidoscope of life that exists in all of the space between us.

Taking stock

Of course, when you have definite proof that your government is lying to you about something so fundamental you start to wonder what else are they lying to you about? You begin to question everything you've been taught about the nature of reality and you learn that it is nearly all a sham and the very worst realisation of all is that our planet is being treated like a farm where all of its creatures are bred, culled and milked according to the wishes of otherworld entities; managed by the shadow

---

[62] Nuts? No doubt some tailwag will be using the term 'barking' about me or this book. They just can't help 'emselves.

servants of the *Darkness,* an elementary force known now as the Devil. Who are these servants? Well they're the people who are involved in covering up this harvest of course including those, whether they know it or not, who are belittling and denying the true nature of reality.

Not all visitors to our dimension come with malign intent and in fact there are many that do what they can to help us. Yet the odds seem impossibly stacked against us because, on the surface we are like the old joke of turkey's voting for Christmas. We revel in and grasp for the trinkets they shake at us while they milk our electrical energies - our psychic abilities, our emotions, our auras - and ravish our bodies. We can't get enough of their chemically laced food and drink, medicines and water etc. We crave their irradiating technology - mobile phones, computers, television, etc. that now *return to sender* everything you do and say. We might look mostly ok but we are all mentally and etherically stumbling around lost until the round up. Today's world is awash with lassos - techniques designed to control how, when and what to think. When *they* want you to be somewhere at a certain time to do something, anything - then you'll be there. I don't intend to get any more political than I have done already but ponder on the implications of this: All terrorism is a product of mind control.

Fears too can be quelled by suggestion as well as technological means of mind control and of course it is possible that some of my experiences have been due to what is known as MILABS - military abductions. The tunnel memory and the helicopter incident might or might not have military involvement for instance. If they are, then I ask myself why? I would suggest that everyone who has an ability to traverse dimensions would certainly be of interest to the military.

People tend to think of hardware and material things when technology is talked about but there are also multidimensional crafts, tools and weapons that exist in realms beyond our senses that we need ultra-computer technology to recognise and to use. I am not a technologically minded person so I can't explain these things though I have seen and been on them. While we might not be able to notice the technology we sometimes can see some of the process. When I was near Area 51 with friends after the UFO conference in Laughlin we saw a test beam bleed-through that took the shape of a smoky thin arc (similar technology is also used to guide aeroplanes; a friend and I saw one guiding a plane that was setting a chemtrail over south Oxfordshire a few years back.

(Chemtrails, for those who don't know, are noxious clouds expelled from quick aircraft that bear a resemblance to ordinary jet aircraft contrails. Whereas contrails are streak-like and disperse very quickly chemtrails are huge coils that sit in the sky for much longer and are mostly laid in grids or patterns. People in the media cannot see them - probably because of their stiff necks.)

As you may have guessed I don't care for what passes for the media; I'm not impressed by their overtures of 'yes but if you come on our show *you are getting your story out, selling books, getting better known* blah-de-blah'. I'm not doing this for any of those reasons.

Why am I doing it then?

Because they are here mate; and it ain't a joke.

May the Goddess bless you with inspiration *and* stardust
and Our Creator with the wisdom *to use them well.*

With Love
Ellis

Acknowledgements

I wish to especially thank my parents for providing me with this opportunity for a human experience full of such wonder. My beautiful partner K who in such a brief time shared so much . . . and stayed - I can't believe my luck!; and all of my friends and family who have walked with and without me through convention's disobedient worlds.

I very much want to mention;

My good friends, visionary artist, Neil Hague for capturing the eerie 'dogs at the door' scene so well for the cover of this book; to Jenny Taylor for her terrific rendition of Botticelli's Venus; and Ann Andrews, Pearl, Michelle Brereton, Paola Harris, Lucy Pringle, Geoff Ambler, Mac and Andrew King for their revealing photographs and diagrams and Debbie Gill for her photograph of Culbone church; Steve Johnson, Geoff Ambler, Ann Andrews, Ben Emlyn-Jones, Ben Fairhall, Mike Oram, Fran Pickering, John Pickering, Katie Hall, Mary Rodwell and Karen Sawyer for being courageous enough to stand with me; and then Mary Rodwell again for, well, being there, for me, my partner and for countless people across the globe who needed someone considerate and trustworthy to talk to about their *contact* experiences. Thank you.

I am so very lucky to have companions and friends such as you.

And before I go . . . My adorable, gorgeous, beautiful children and grandchildren: you are my dreams come true.

This book is also available with colour pictures.

I am also considering publishing, in the future, a companion book, maybe an EBook, that will have just colour photographs as well as a Dogged Days photo section on my website.
www.ellisctaylor.com

Ellis Taylor
Living in the Matrix
Another Way
Numerology for a New Day

Available from
BiggyBoo Books, UK

ISBN 978-0-9550417-1-6

&
Hidden Mysteries in the USA

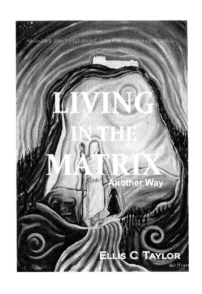

Ellis Taylor
IN THESE SIGNS CONQUER
Revealing the secret signs
an Age has obscured

Available from:
BiggyBoo Books, UK

ISBN: 978-0-95568-610-8

&
Hidden Mysteries in the USA
ISBN: 0-9786249-2-0

Ellis Taylor
**IN THESE SIGNS
CONQUER**
Revealing the secret signs
an Age has obscured

HARDCOVER

BiggyBoo Books, UK

ISBN: 978-0-9556861-1-5

www.biggyboo.com

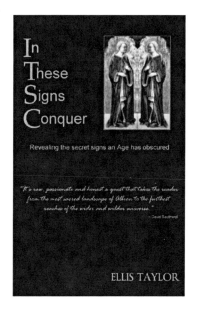

Ellis Taylor
The Esoteric Alphabet

Available from
BiggyBoo Books, UK

www.biggyboo.com

Further Reading

Allan, Brian J. *The Hole in the Sky*, Hidden Mysteries, Texas, 2007

Andrews, Ann & Ritchie, J. *Abduction, the true story of Alien Abduction in rural England* Headline Books, London, 1998

Andrews, Ann, *Walking Between Worlds, Belonging to None*, Reality Press, 2007

Broadhurst, Paul & Miller, Hamish, *The Sun and the Serpent, A journey of discovery through the British landscape, its mythology, ancient sites and mysteries*, Pendragon Press, 1989

Cairns, Jim, *Disappeared off the Face of the Earth*, JC Publications, Ireland, 2002

Cooper, William, *Behold A Pale Horse*, Light Technology Publishing, Arizona, 1991

de Vere, Nicholas, *The Dragon Legacy*, The Book Tree, Santiago, 2004

Cowan, David R. & Chris Arnold, *Ley Lines and Earth Energies*, Adventures Unlimited Press 2003

DeCamp, John W, *The Franklin Cover-up*, AWT Inc, Nebraska, 1992

Dodd, Tony, Alien Investigator, Headline Books, London, 1999

Gardner, Laurence, Bloodline of the Holy Grail, The Hidden Lineage of Jesus Revealed, Element Books, 1996

Gardner, Laurence, *Realm of the Ringlords, the Ancient Legacy of the Ring and the Grail*, Element Books,2000

Hague, Neil, *Through Ancient Eyes, Seeing hidden dimensions exploring art and soul connections*, Quester Publications, 2002

Hague, Neil, *Journeys in the Dreamtime, Keys to Unlocking the Imagination Exposing the Untold History of Art,* Quester Publications, 2006

Hall, Katie & Pickering, John, *Beyond Photography, Encounters with orbs, angels and mysterious light-forms*, O Books, UK, 2006

Hancock, Graham, *Supernatural*, Century 2005

Harris, Paola Leopizzi, *Connecting the Dots*, Authorhouse 2007

Miles, David, *The Tribes of Britain*, Orion Books, 2006

Mott, Wm. Michael, *Caverns, Cauldrons and Concealed Creatures,* Hidden Mysteries, Texas, 2002

Muir, A&D, *Forrest Family*, 1982

Oram, Mike, *Does It Rain in Other Dimensions?*, O Books, UK, 2007

Power, Andrew, *Ireland, Land of the Pharaohs, The Quest for our Atlantean Legacy*, Peninsular Print, Ireland, 2005

Rodwell, Mary, *Awakening, How ET Contact can Transform your life!* Avatar Publications, Alberta 2002

Sawyer, Karen, *Soul companions, Conversations with contemporary wisdom keepers - a collection of encounters with spirit*, O Books, UK, 2008

Sitchin, Zecharia, The Earth Chronicles, Harper; First Avon Books Edition, 1978

Smith, Yvonne, *Chosen: Recollections of UFO Abductions Through Hypnotherapy,* Backstage Entertainment, 2008

Southwell, David & Twist, Sean, *Conspiracy Files*, Carlton Books, London, 2007

Southwell, David, *Secrets and Lies, Exposing the World of Cover-Ups and Deception,* Carlton, London, 2005

Talbot, Michael, *The Holographic Universe*, Harper Collins, 1991

Taylor, Ellis, *Living in the Matrix, Another Way, Numerology for a New Day,* BiggyBoo Books, Oxford, UK & Hidden Mysteries, USA, 2005

Taylor, Ellis, *In These Signs Conquer, Revealing the secret signs an Age has obscured,* BiggyBoo Books, Oxford, UK & Hidden Mysteries, USA, 2006

Tsarion, Michael, *Atlantis, Alien Visitation & Genetic Manipulation,* Personal Transformation Press, California, 2002

Waddell, L.A. *The British Edda*, Christian Book Club, California, 1930

Websites

Ellis Taylor,	www.ellisctaylor.com
ACERN E.T. Experiencer support (Australia)	www.acern.com
Ann Andrews	www.walkingbetweenworlds.co.uk
Anomalist News	www.anomalist.com
Bagoll the Traveller	www.cryearth.com
Ben Emlyn-Jones	http://hpanwo.blogspot.com
Ben Fairhall	www.benfairhall.com
Bully OnLine	www.bullyonline.org
Contact International UFO Research	http://contactinternationalufo.homestead.com
Cornwall UFO Group	www.cornwall-ufo.co.uk
Crop Circle Connector	www.cropcircleconnector.com
David Cowan Dowsing etc	www.leyman.demon.co.uk
David Sandercock & Rochelle D'Elia	www.elkmusic.com
David Southwell	www.davidsouthwell.com
E-Clips Institute Alien Abduction Information (UK)	www.e-clipsinstitute.org
Harmonic Blueprint	www.harmonicblueprint.com
Hidden Mysteries	www.hiddenmysteries.com
Irish UFO Society	www.ufosocietyireland.com
James Casbolt	www.jamescasbolt.com
Katie Hall & John Pickering (orbs)	www.lights2beyond.com
Lucy Pringle (Crop Circle research)	www.lucypringle.co.uk
Malcolm Robinson (researcher)	www.myspace.com/malcolmrobinsonresearcher
Mark Townsend (magician/illusionist)	www.magicofsoul.com
Matthew Delooze	www.matthewdelooze.co.uk
Mercury Rapids (Steve Johnson)	www.mercuryrapids.co.uk
Mike Oram	www.inotherdimensions.com
Mind Motivations (All about Hypnosis)	www.mindmotivations.com
Neil Hague, *Visionary Artist and Writer*,	www.neilhague.com
Michael Tsarion	www.michaeltsarion.com
Missing Persons (Ireland)	www.missingpersons-ireland.freepress-freespeech.com
New Zealand UFO Research	www.ufocusnz.org.nz
Nubian Time	www.nubiantime.com
Occult of Personality	http://rochester92.vox.com
Oxfordshire Centre for Crop Circle Studies	www.oxfordshirecropcircles.co.uk
Paola Harris	www.paolaharris.com
Paranormal Encounters Group	www.p-e-g.co.uk
Philip Gardiner	www.gardinersworld.com
Project Camelot	www.projectcamelot.net
PROBE International (conferences)	www.ukprobe.com
Ross Hemsworth (presenter)	www.myspace.com/rosshemsworth
Soul Companions	www.soulcompanions.org
Stuart Wilde	www.stuartwilde.com
The Anomalist	http://anomalist.com
The British Society of Dowsers	www.britishdowsers.org
The Daily Grail	www.dailygrail.com
The Humanitad Foundation	www.humanitad.org
The International Society of Dowsers	http://dowsingworks.com
The Irish UFO Society	www.ufosocietyireland.com
The Truth Movement, Australia	www.truthmovementaustralia.com.au
Tracey Taylor, *Visionary Artist*	www.harmonicblueprint.com
UFO Data Magazine,	www.ufodata.co.uk
Yvonne Smith Experiencer support	www.ysmith.com

Printed in the United Kingdom
by Lightning Source UK Ltd.
136389UK00001B/283-294/P